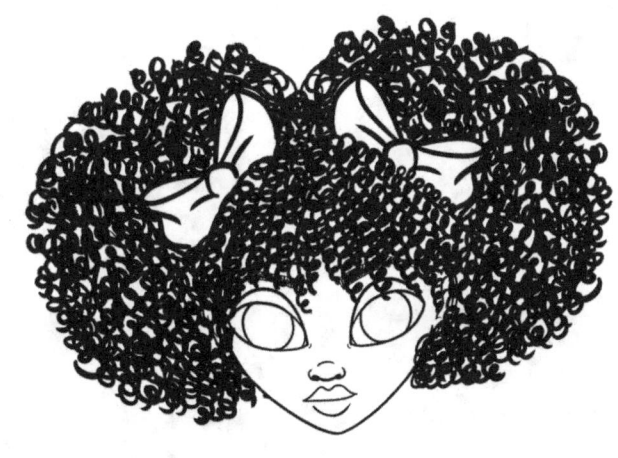

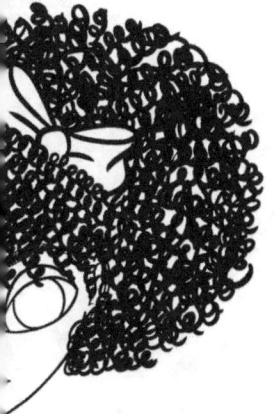

Know Yourself

by Jacqui C. Smith

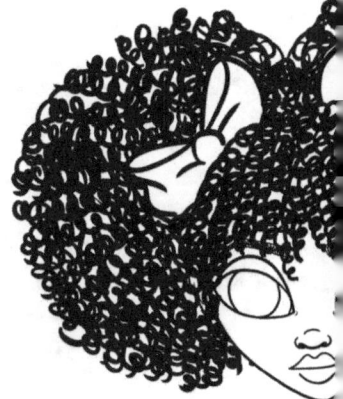

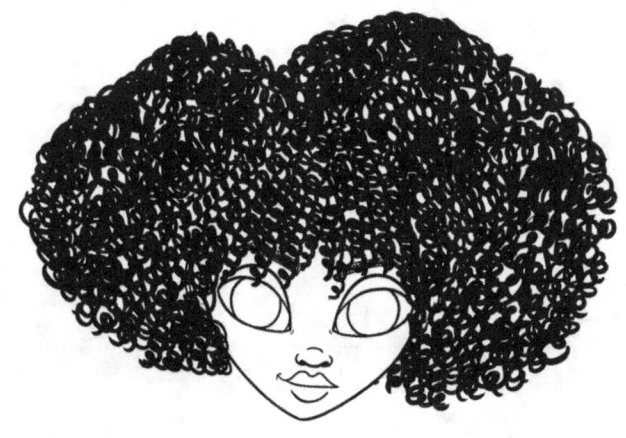
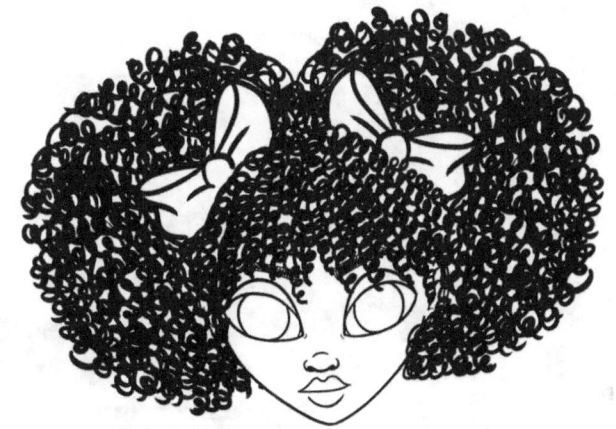

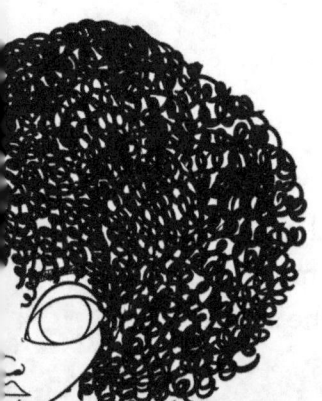
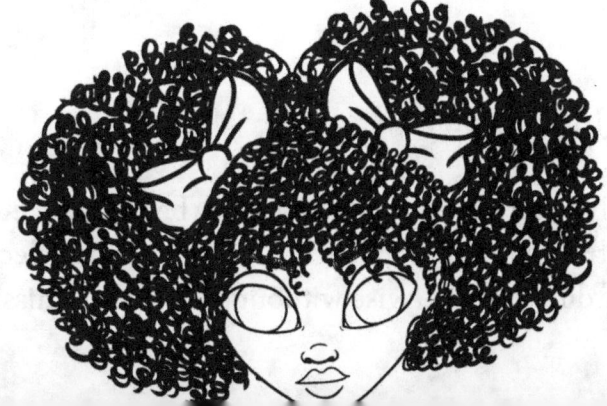
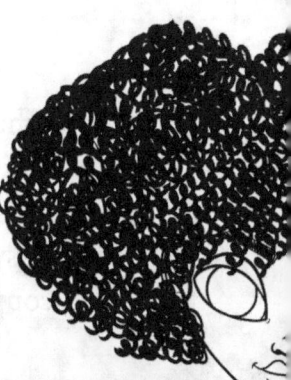

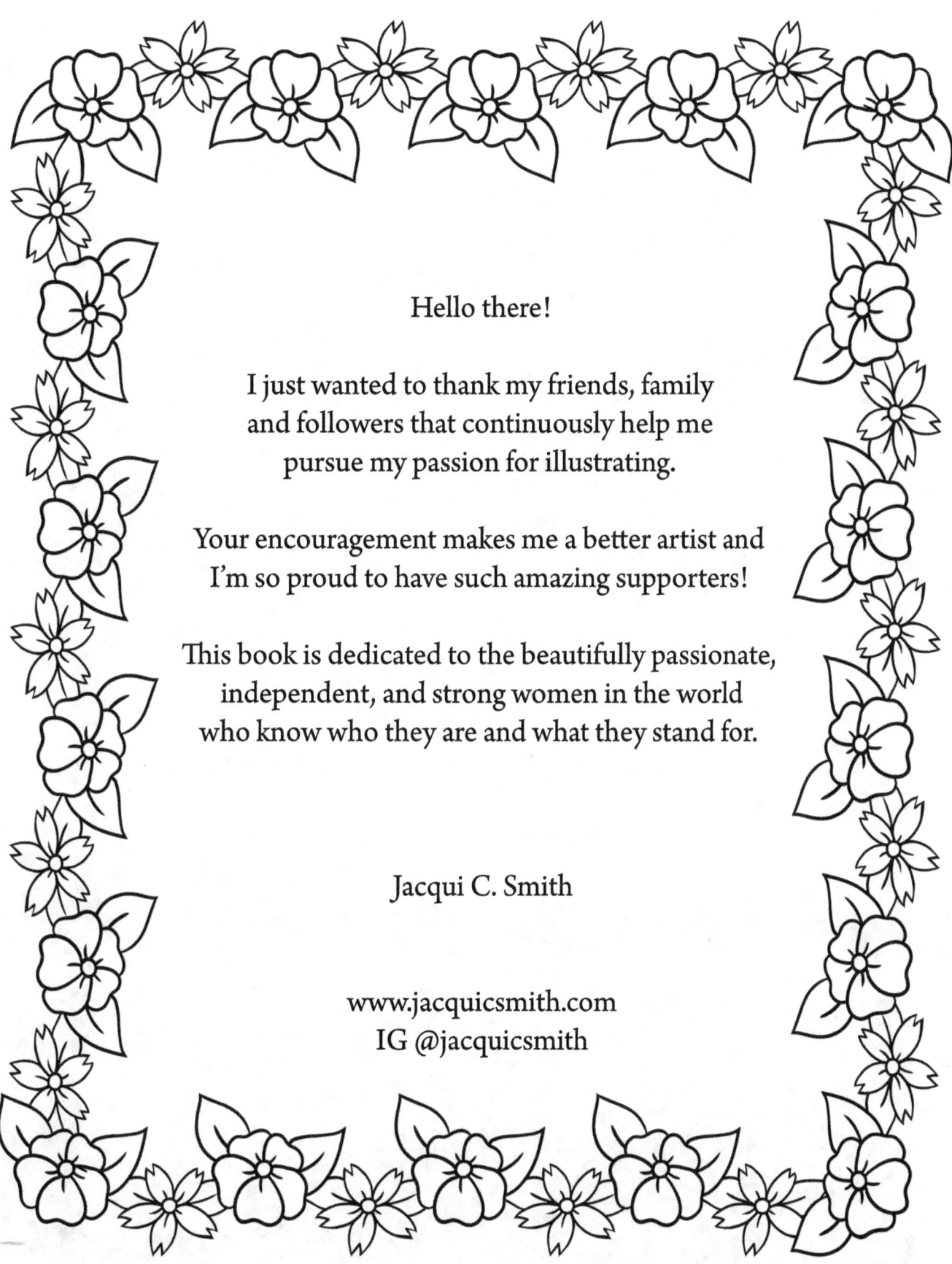

Hello there!

I just wanted to thank my friends, family
and followers that continuously help me
pursue my passion for illustrating.

Your encouragement makes me a better artist and
I'm so proud to have such amazing supporters!

This book is dedicated to the beautifully passionate,
independent, and strong women in the world
who know who they are and what they stand for.

Jacqui C. Smith

www.jacquicsmith.com
IG @jacquicsmith

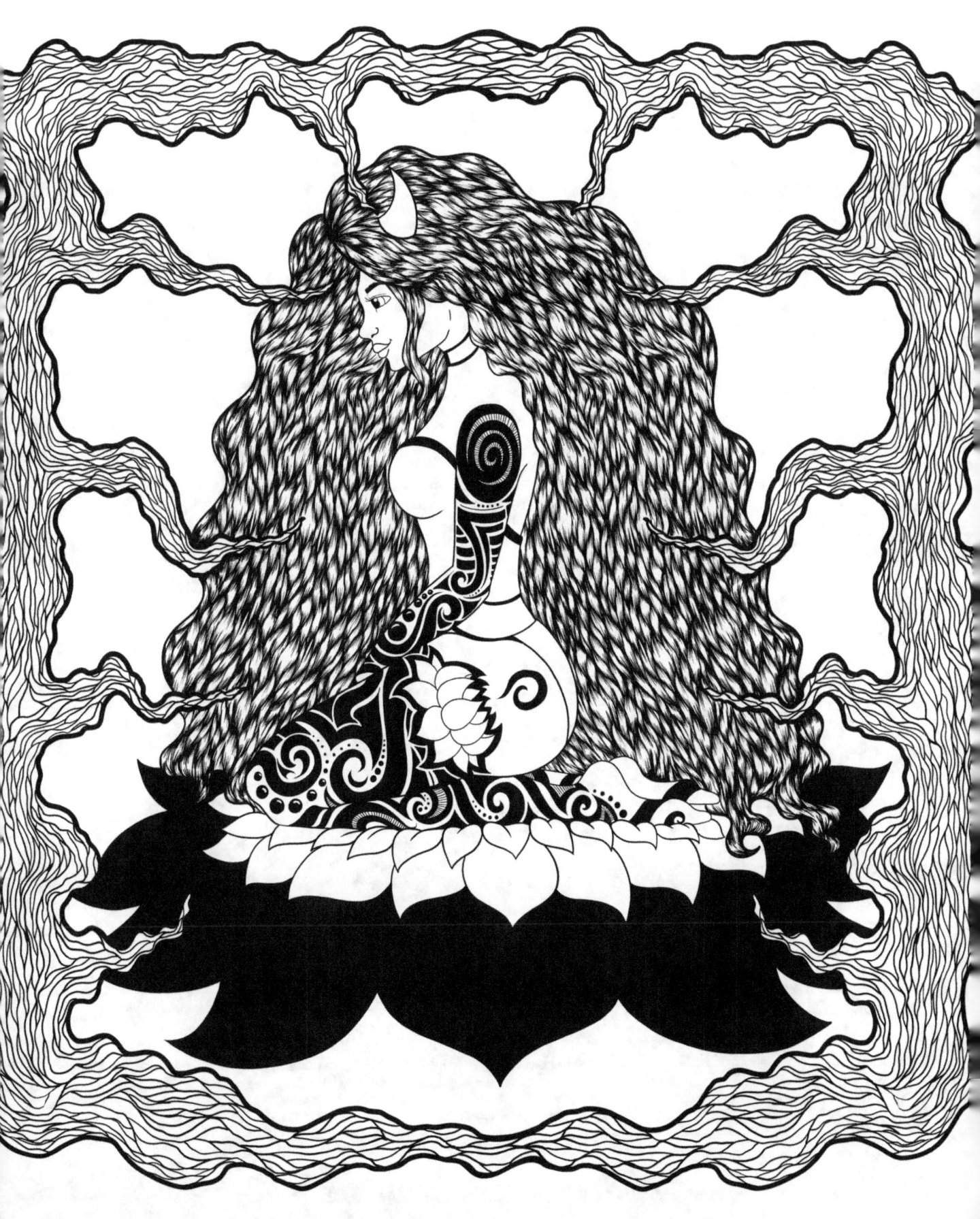

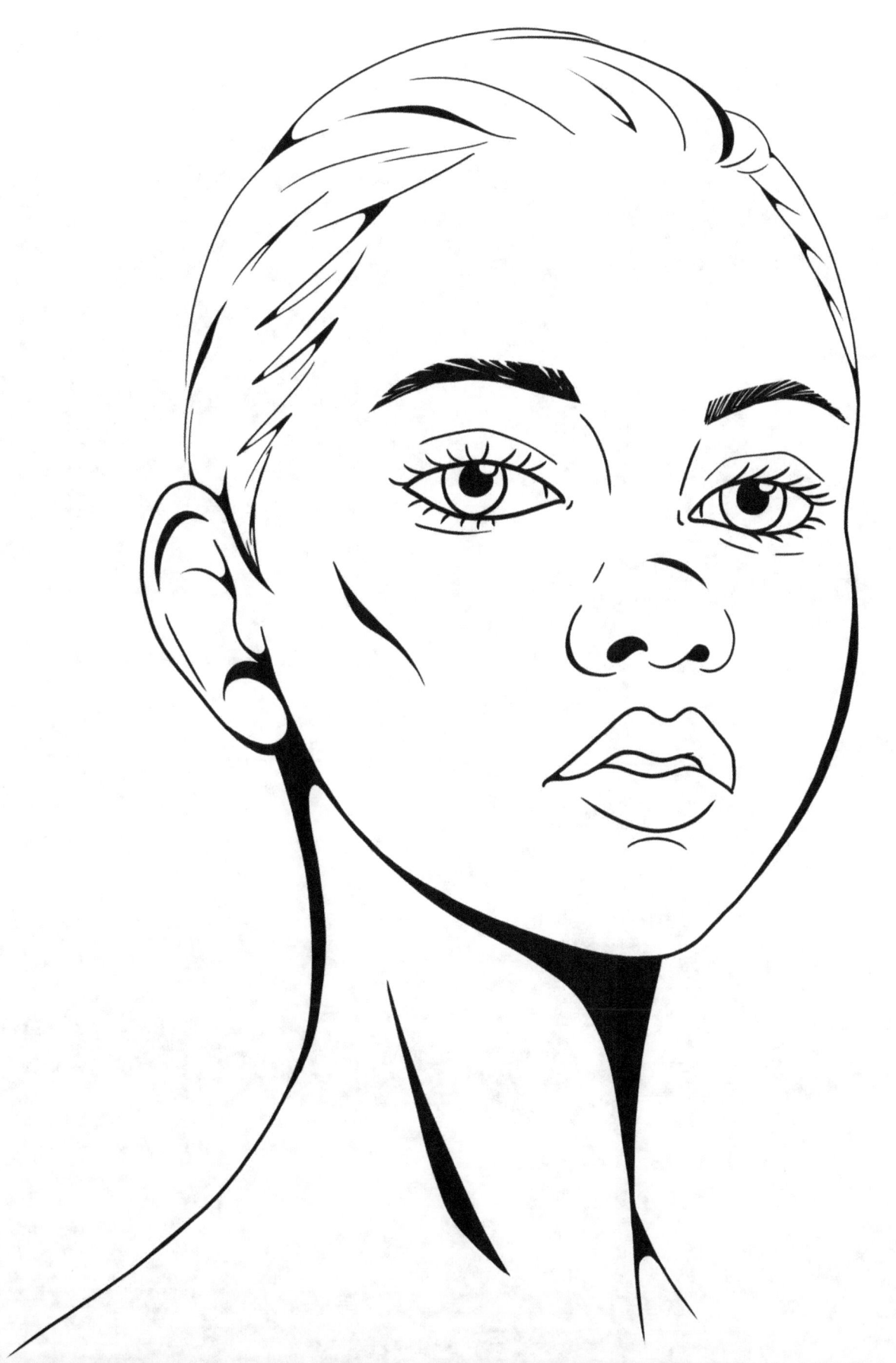

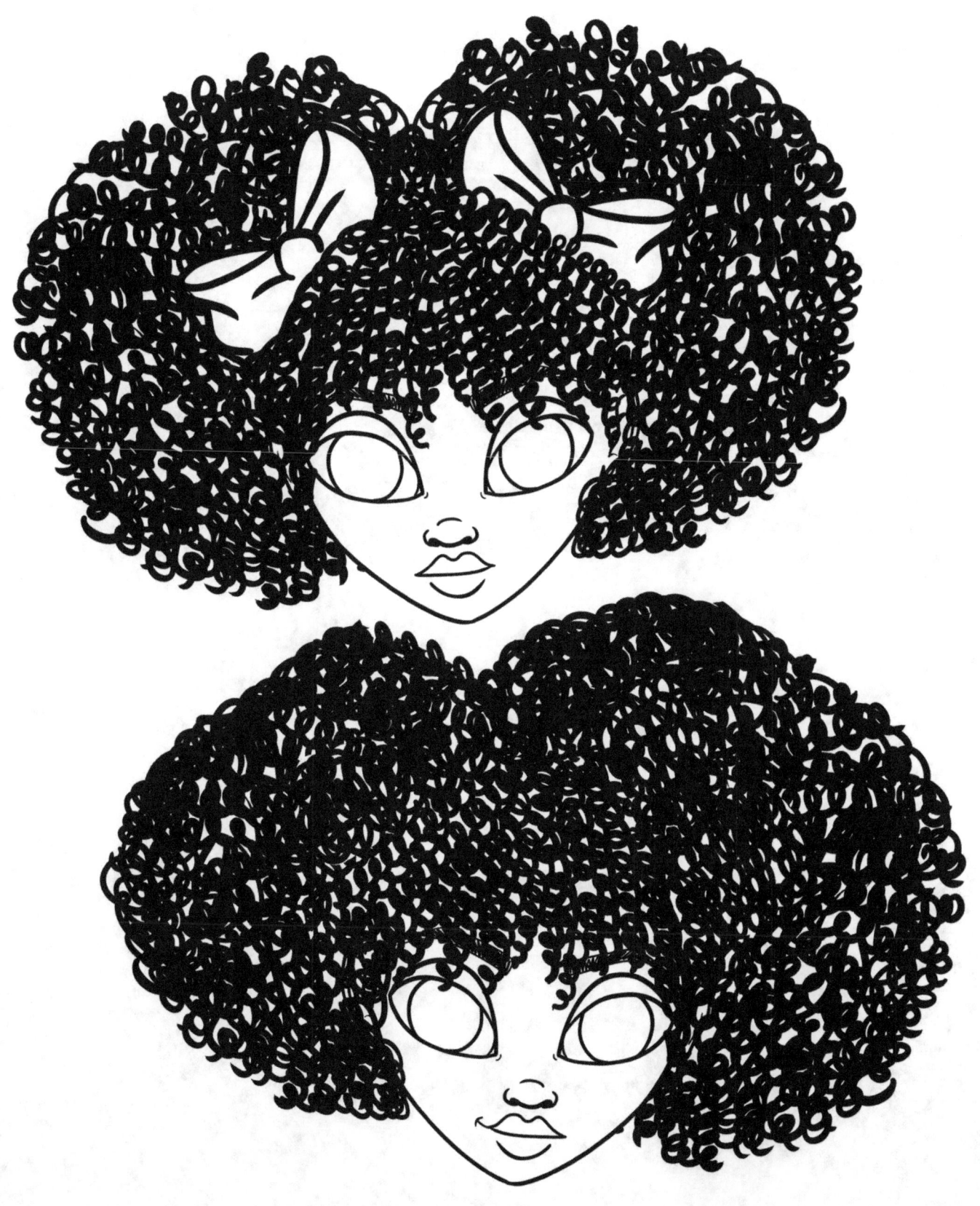

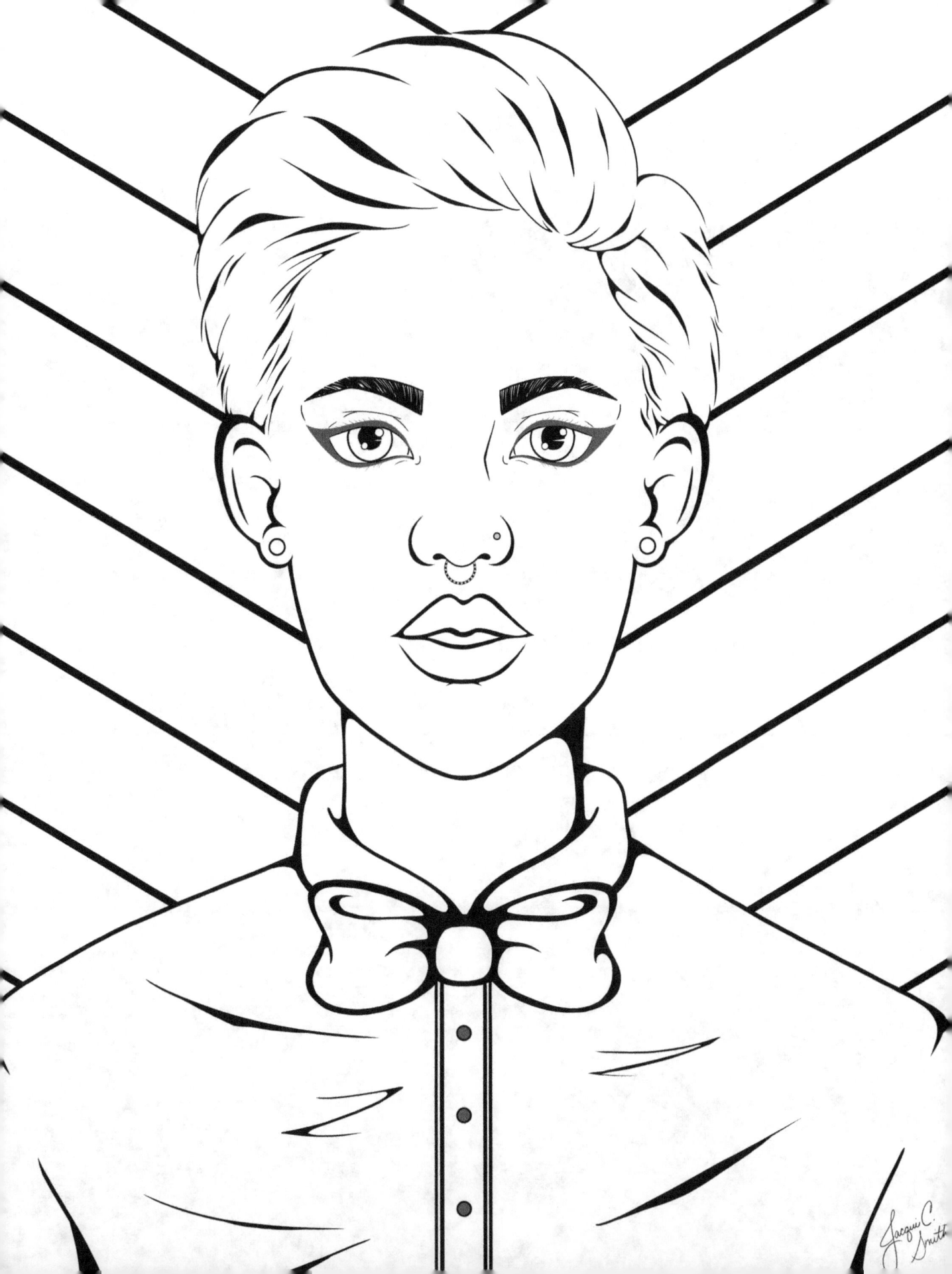

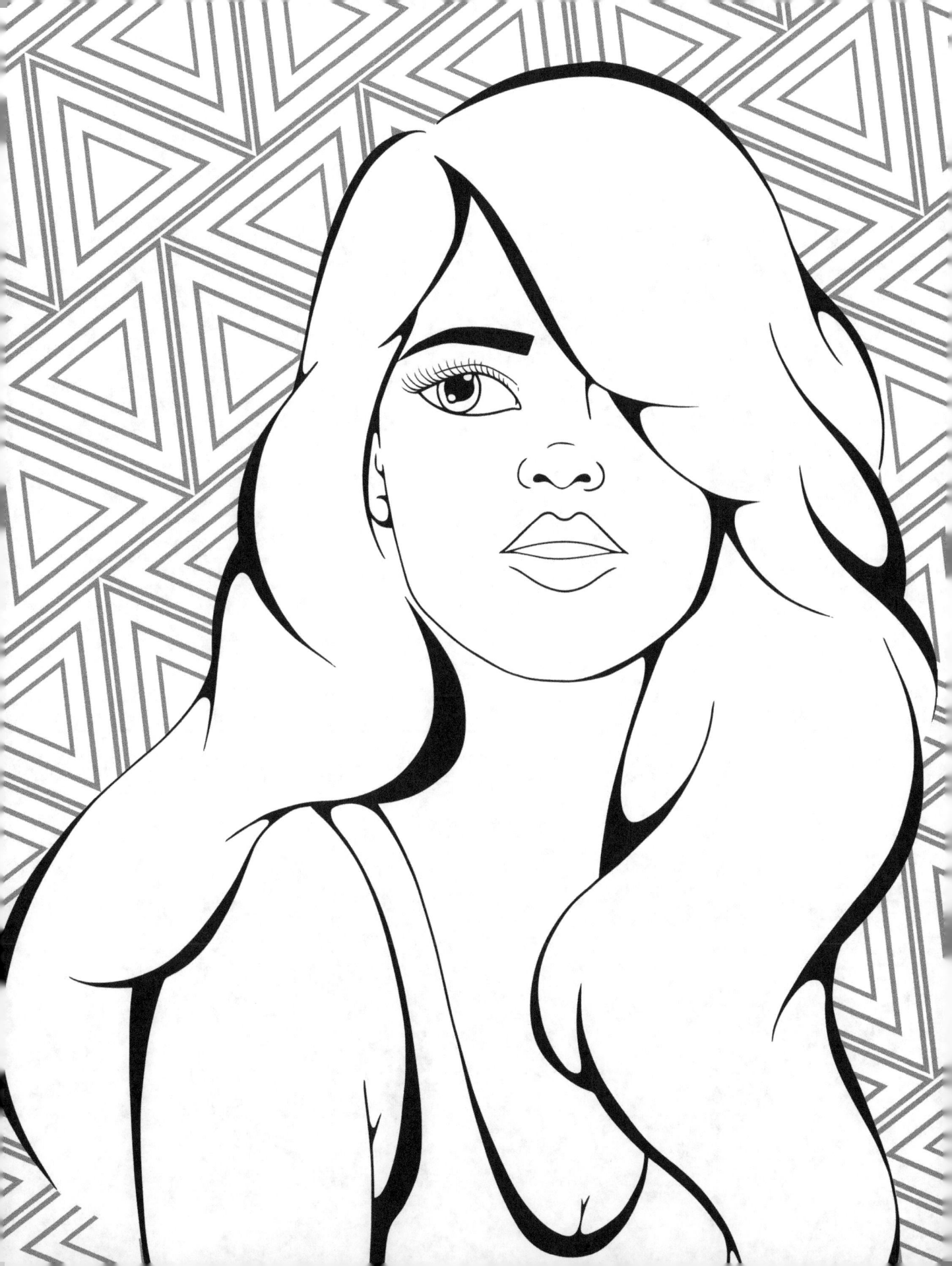

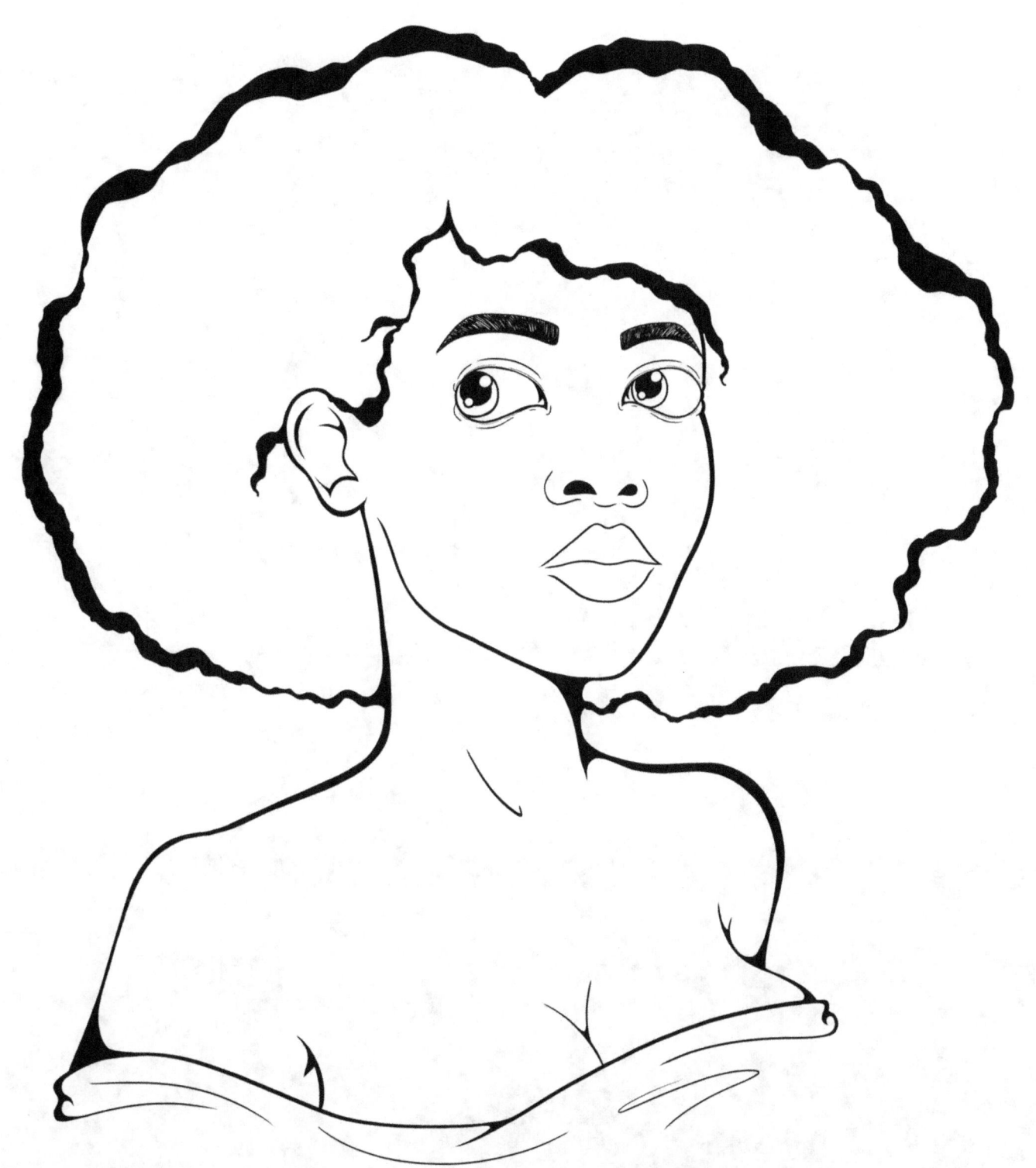

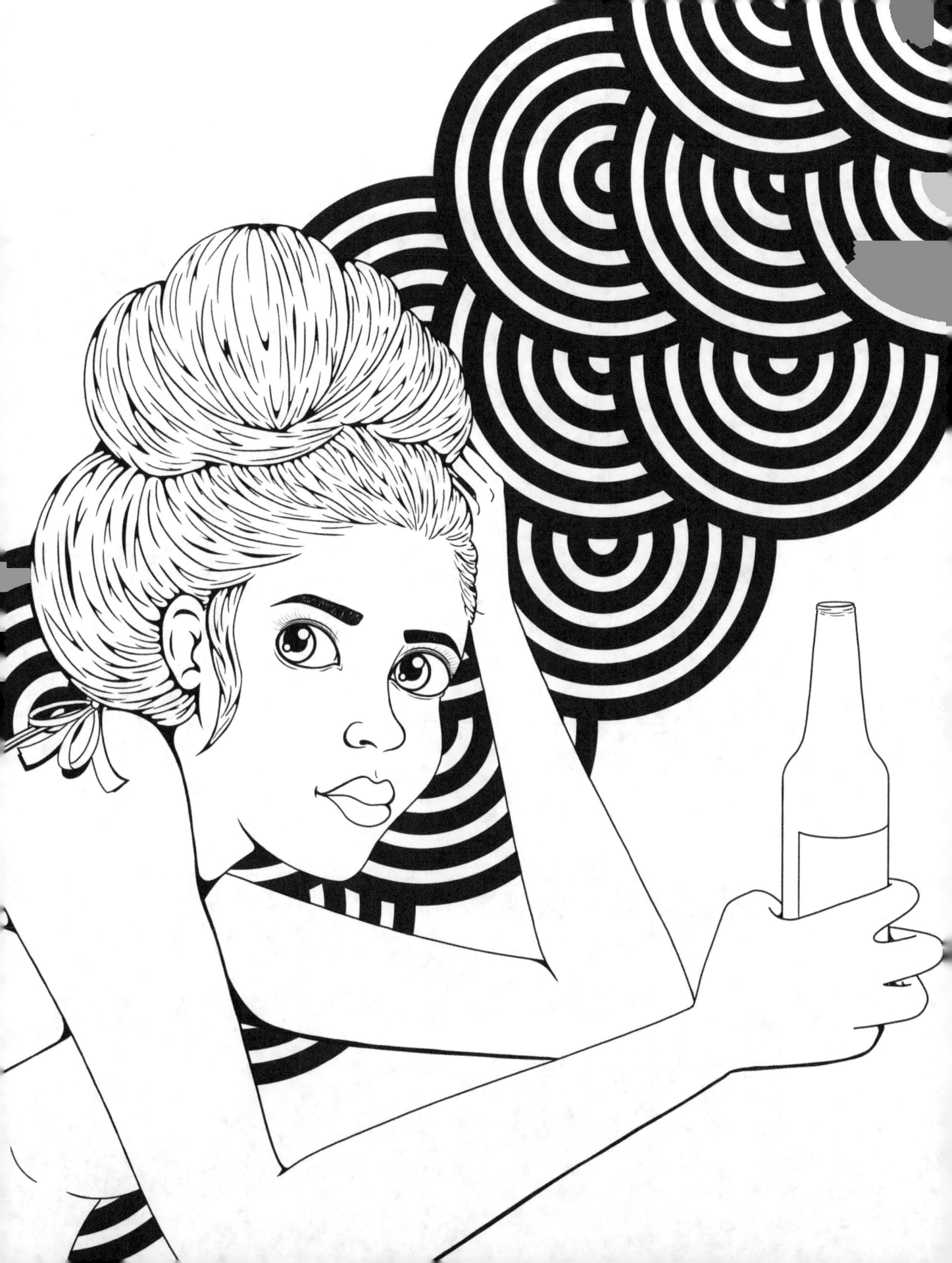

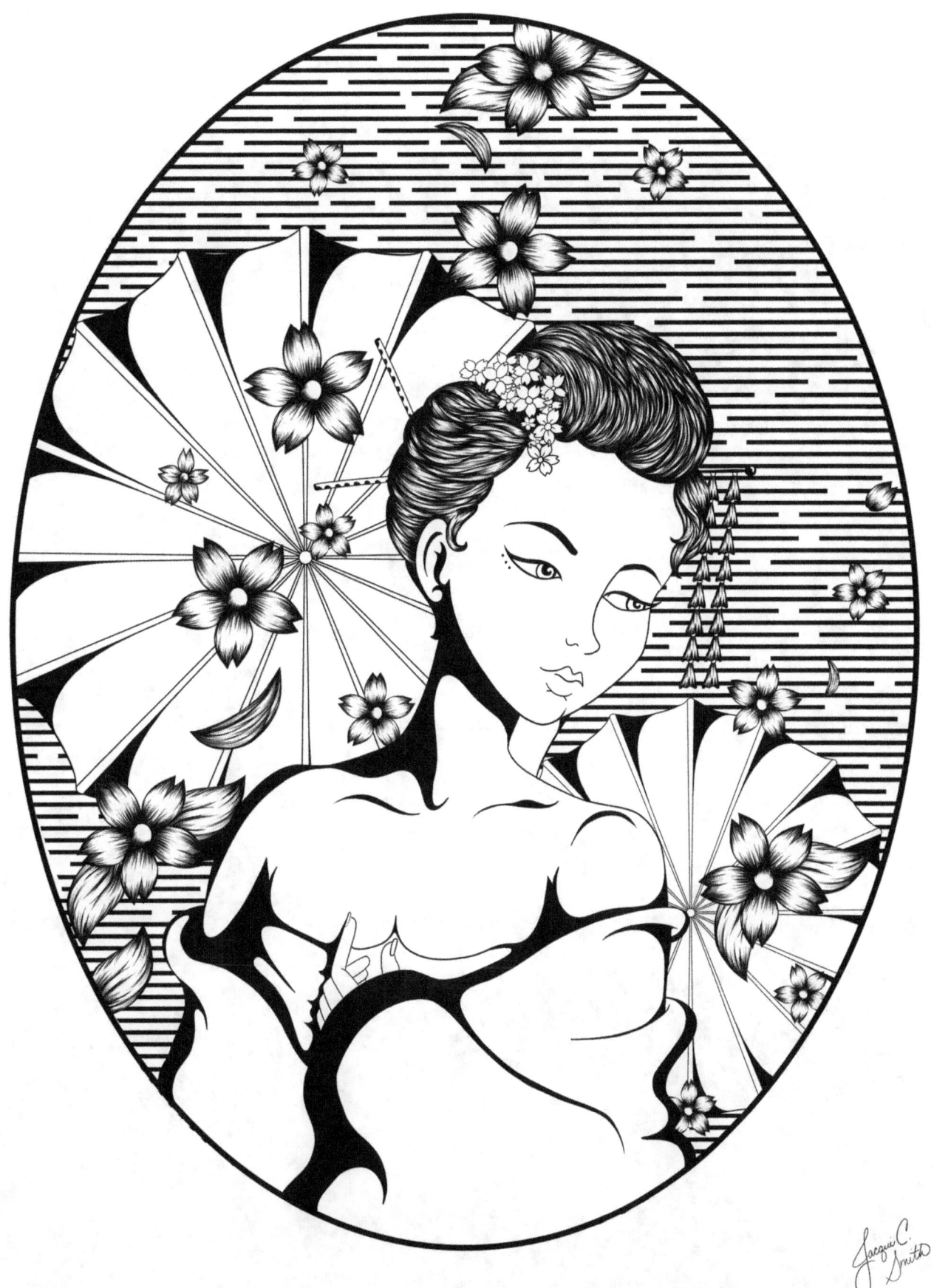

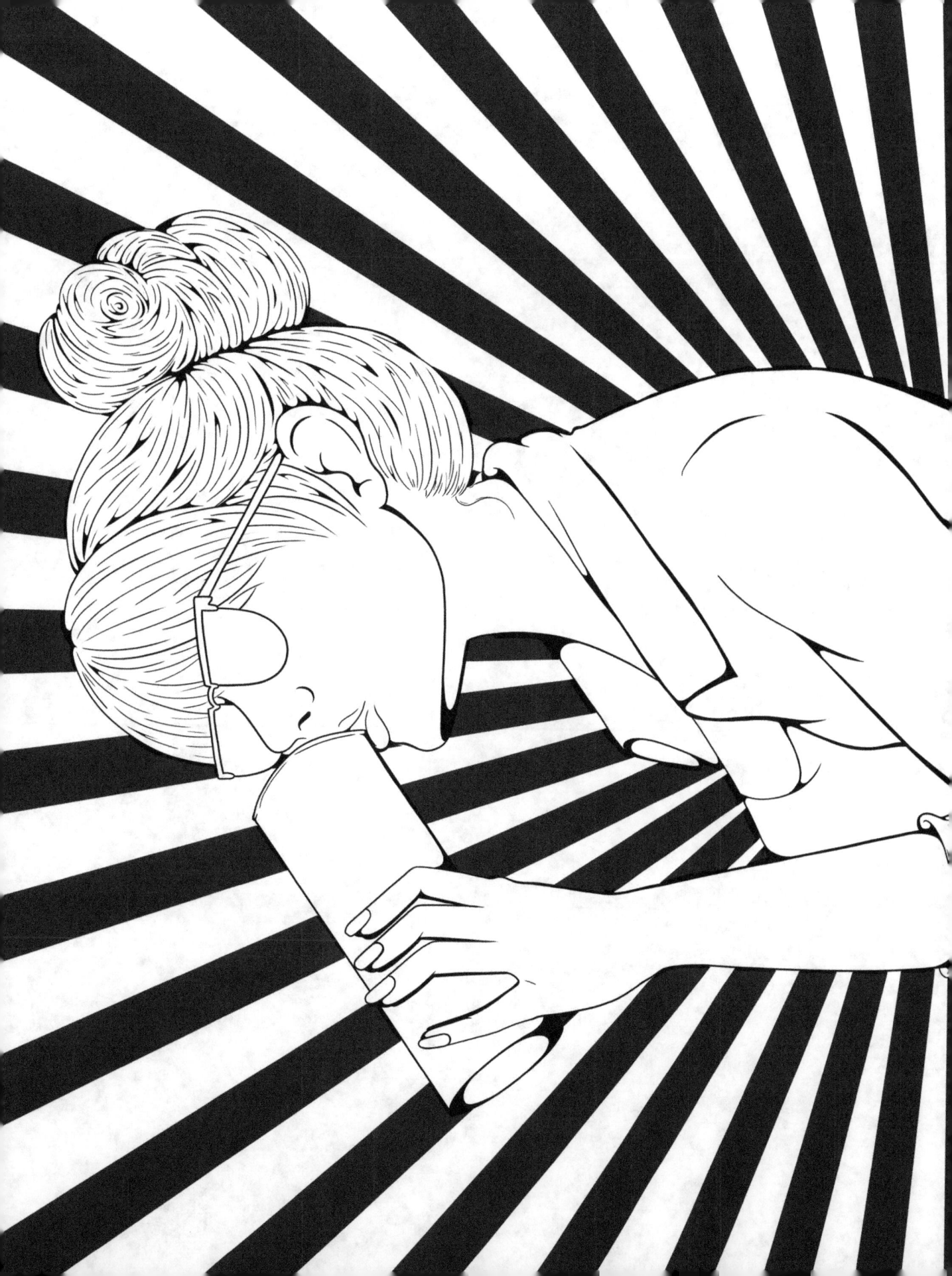

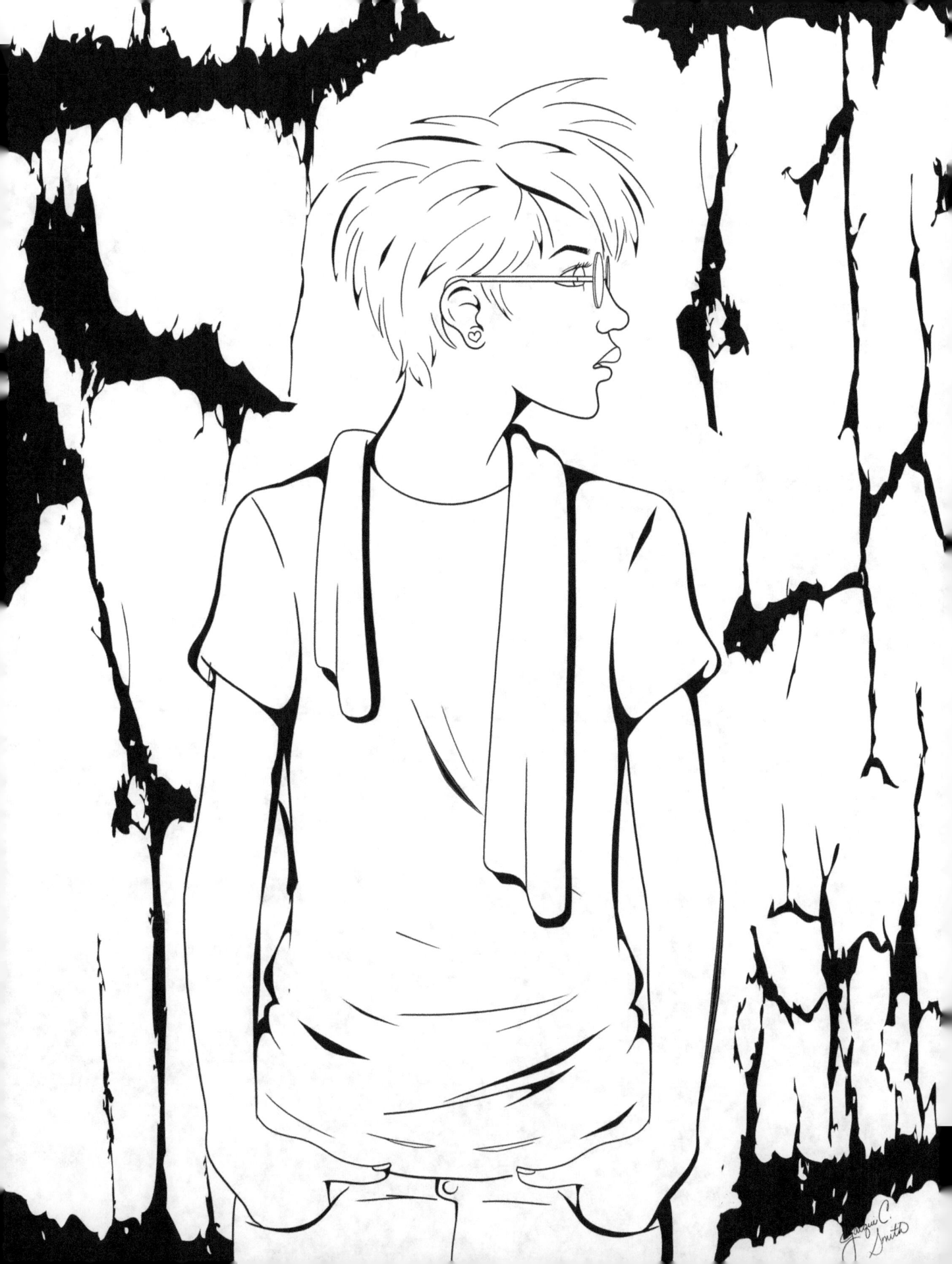

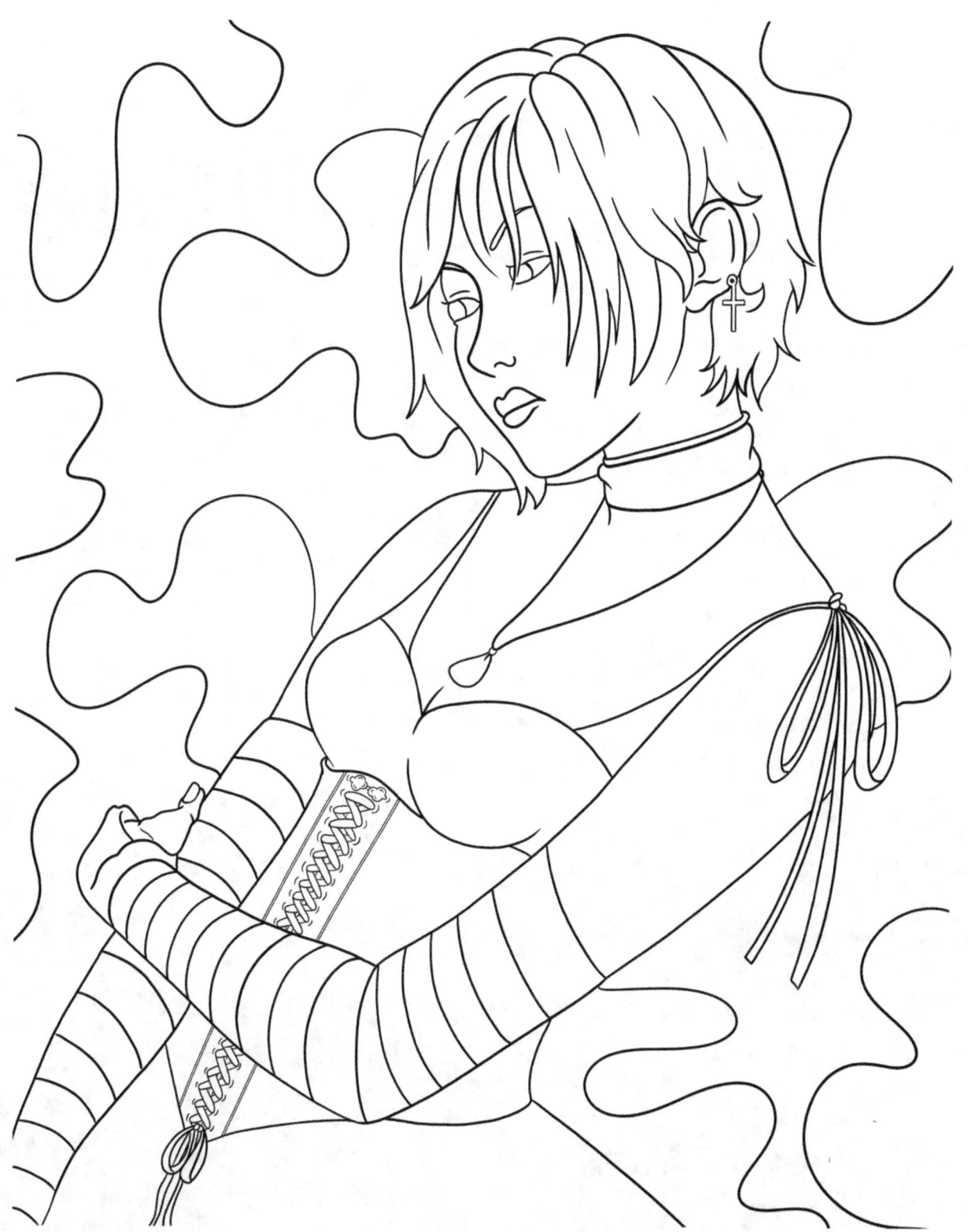

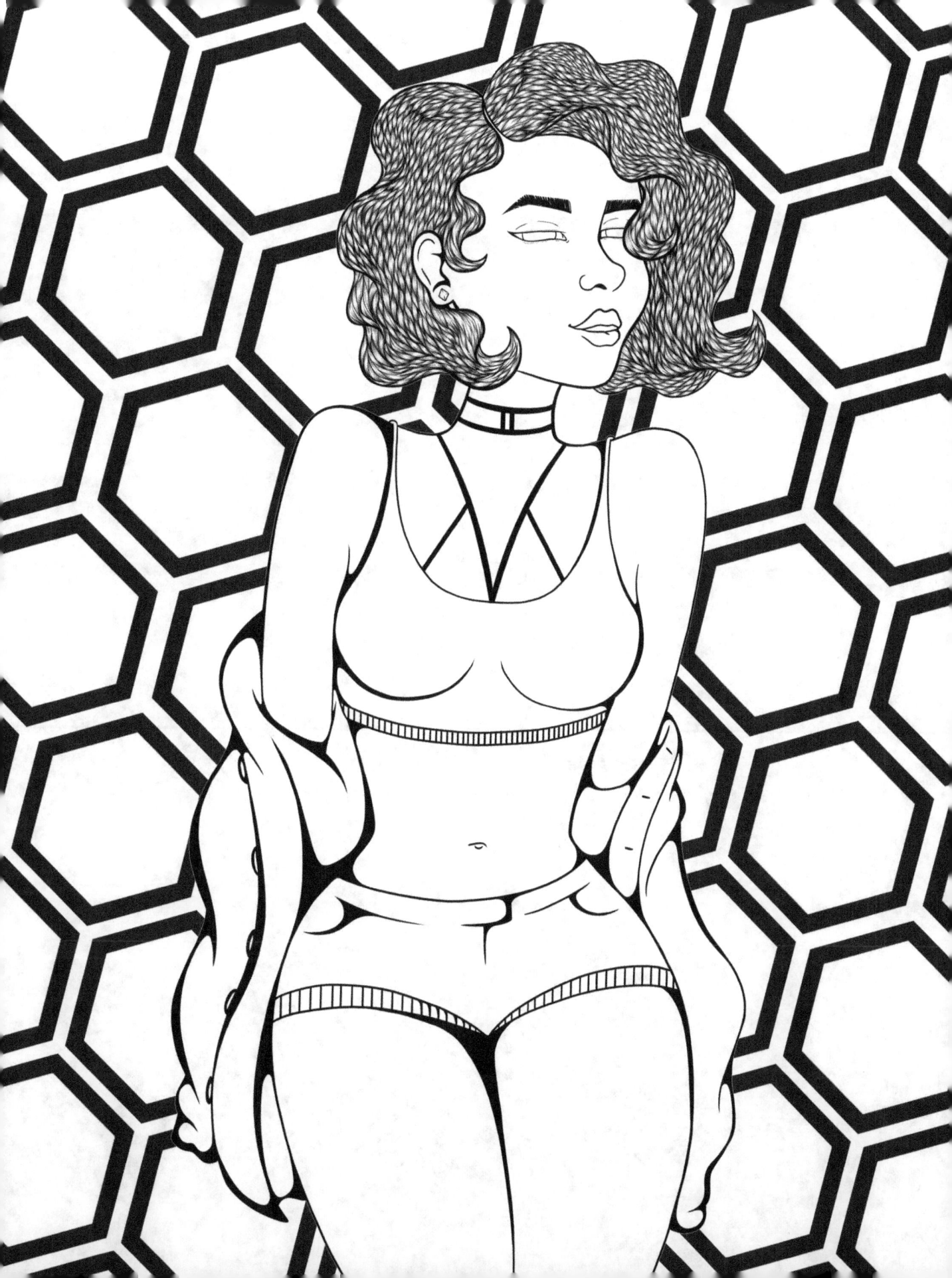

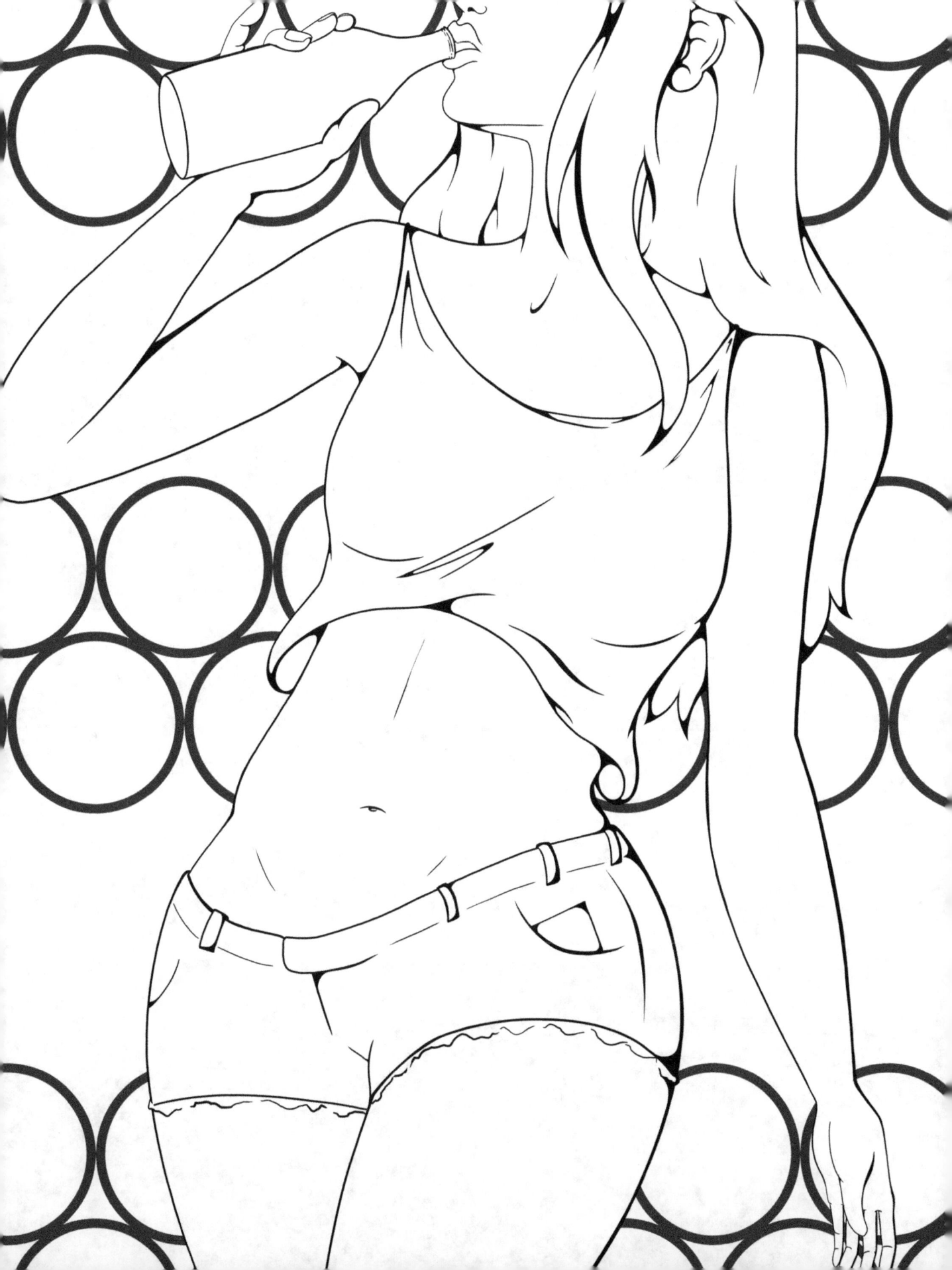

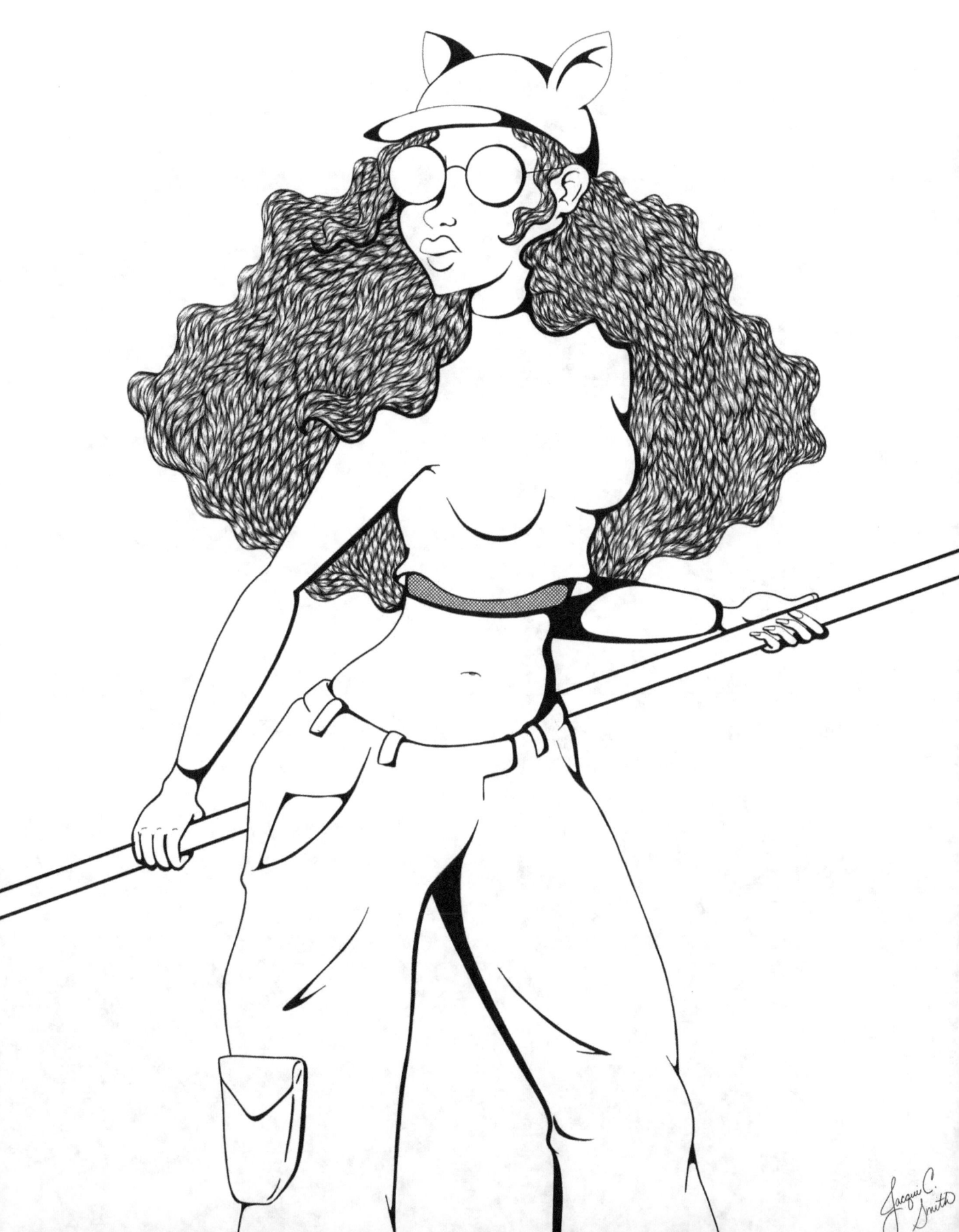

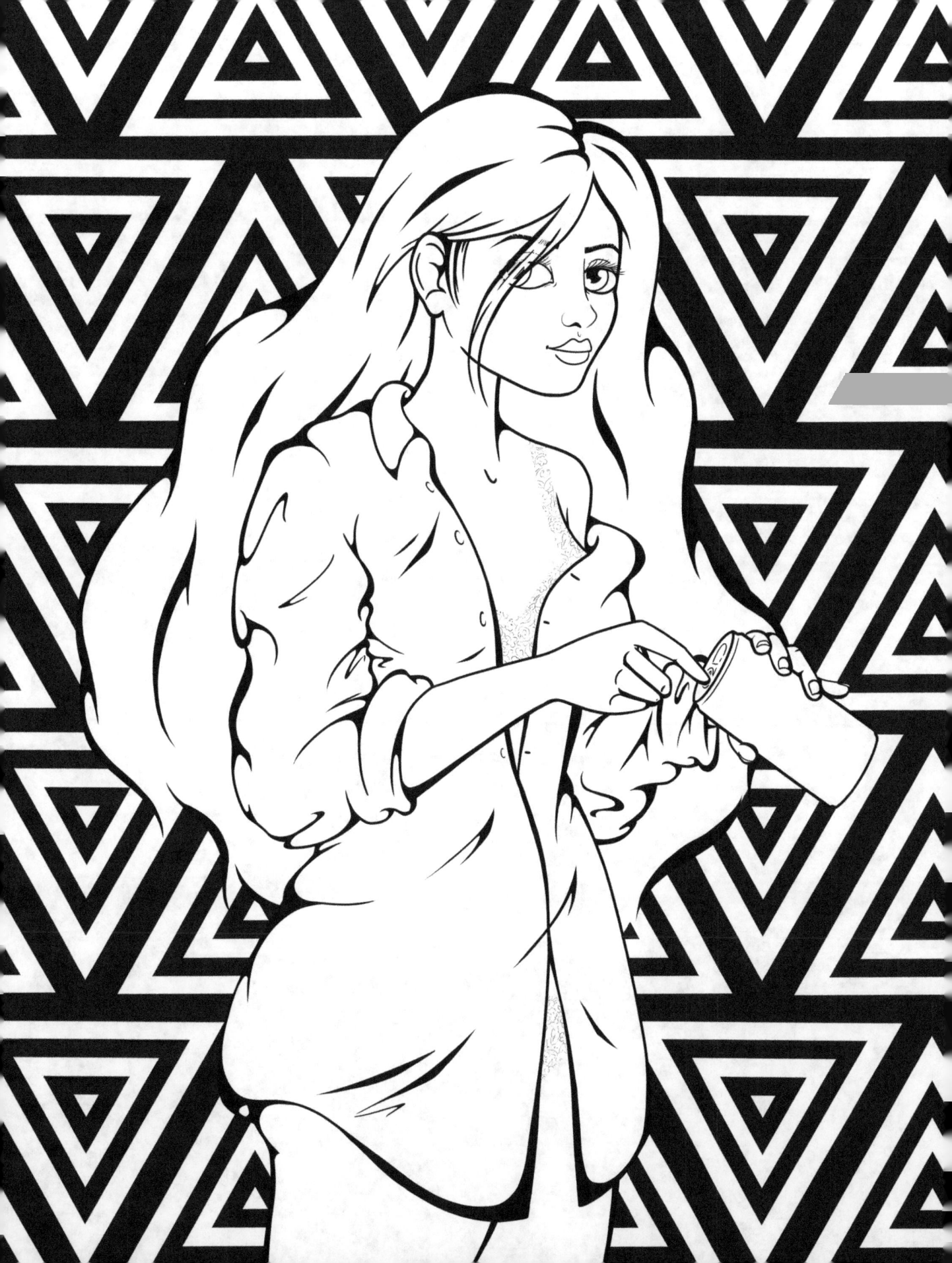

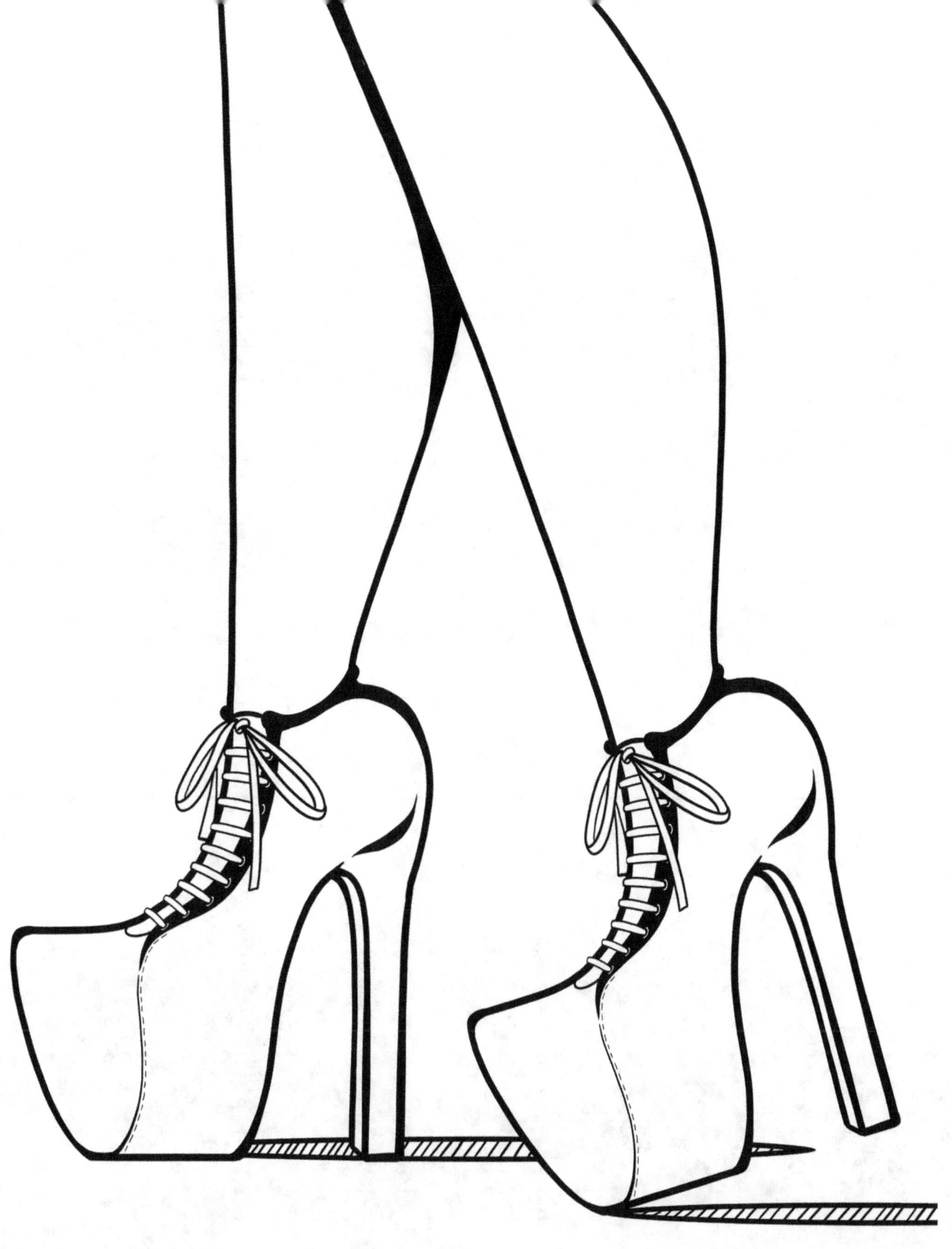

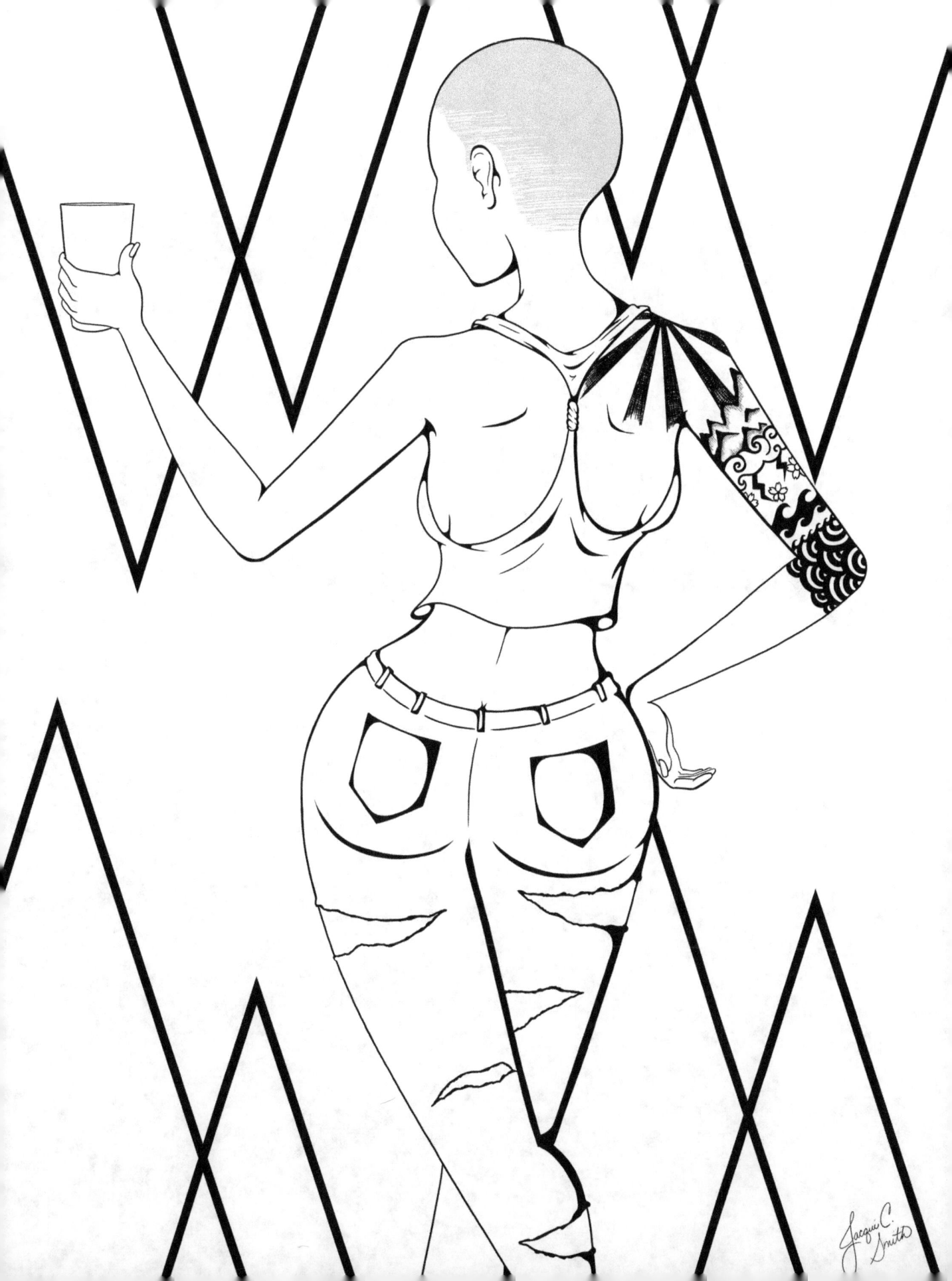

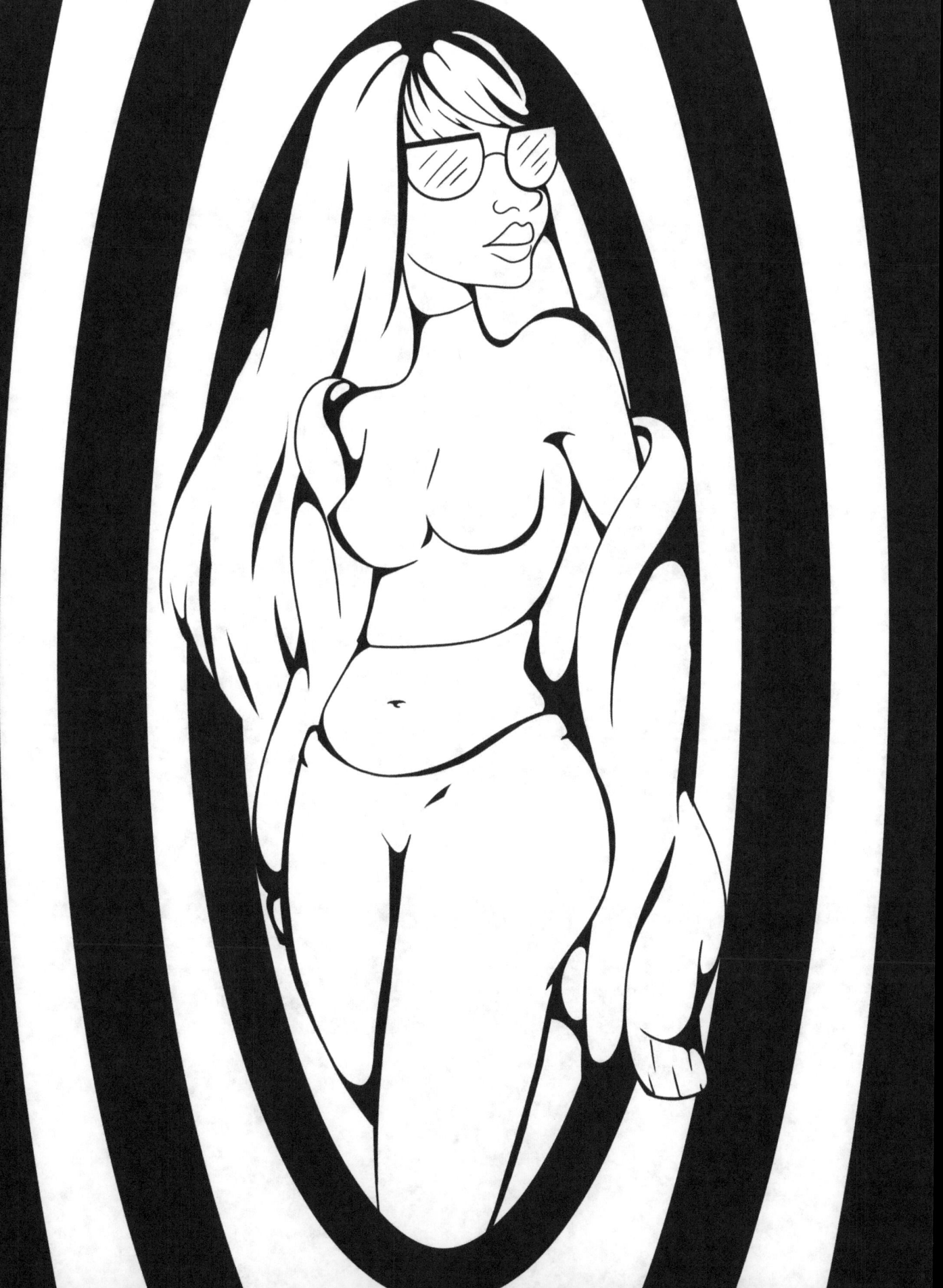

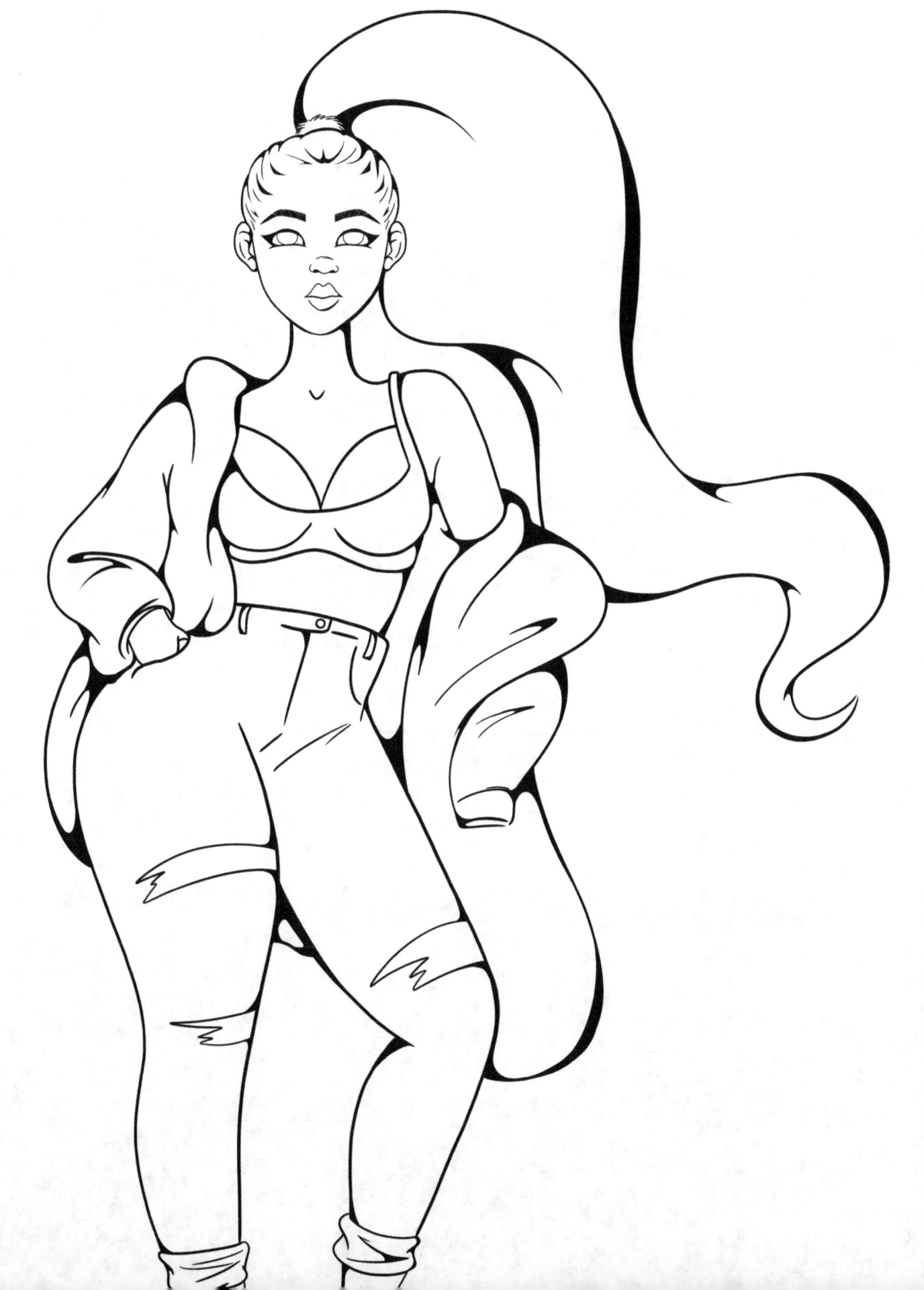

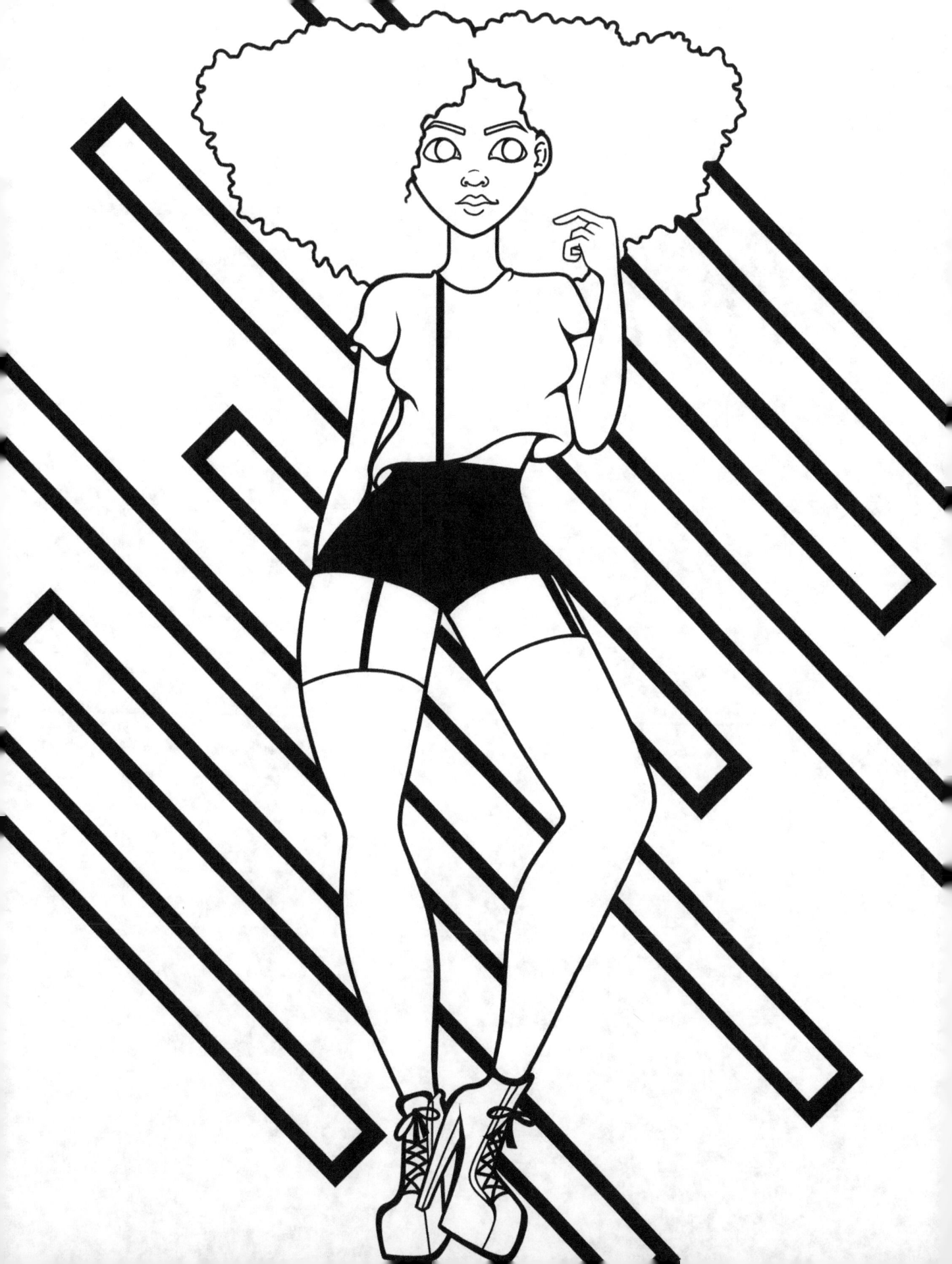

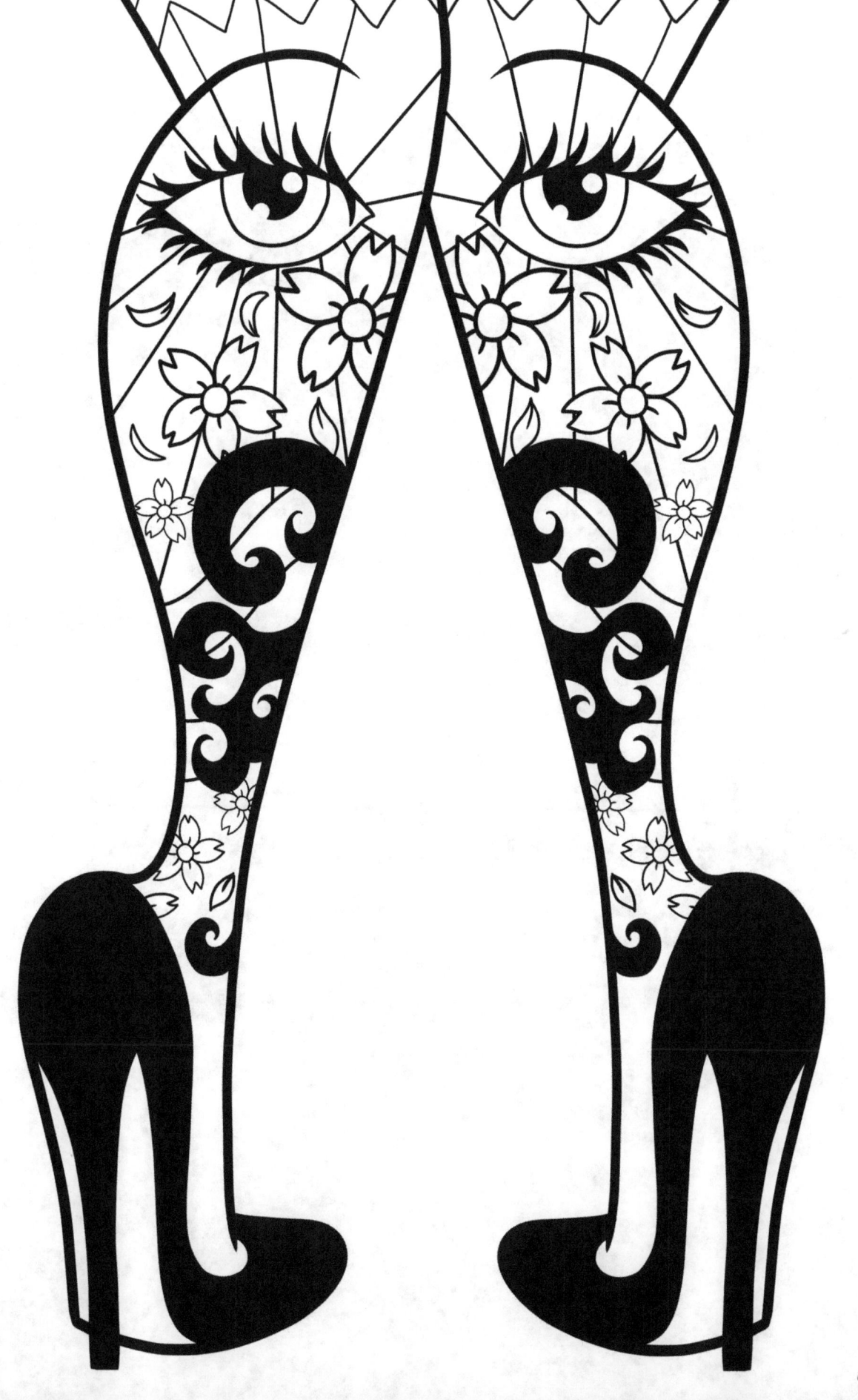

Jacqui C. Smith

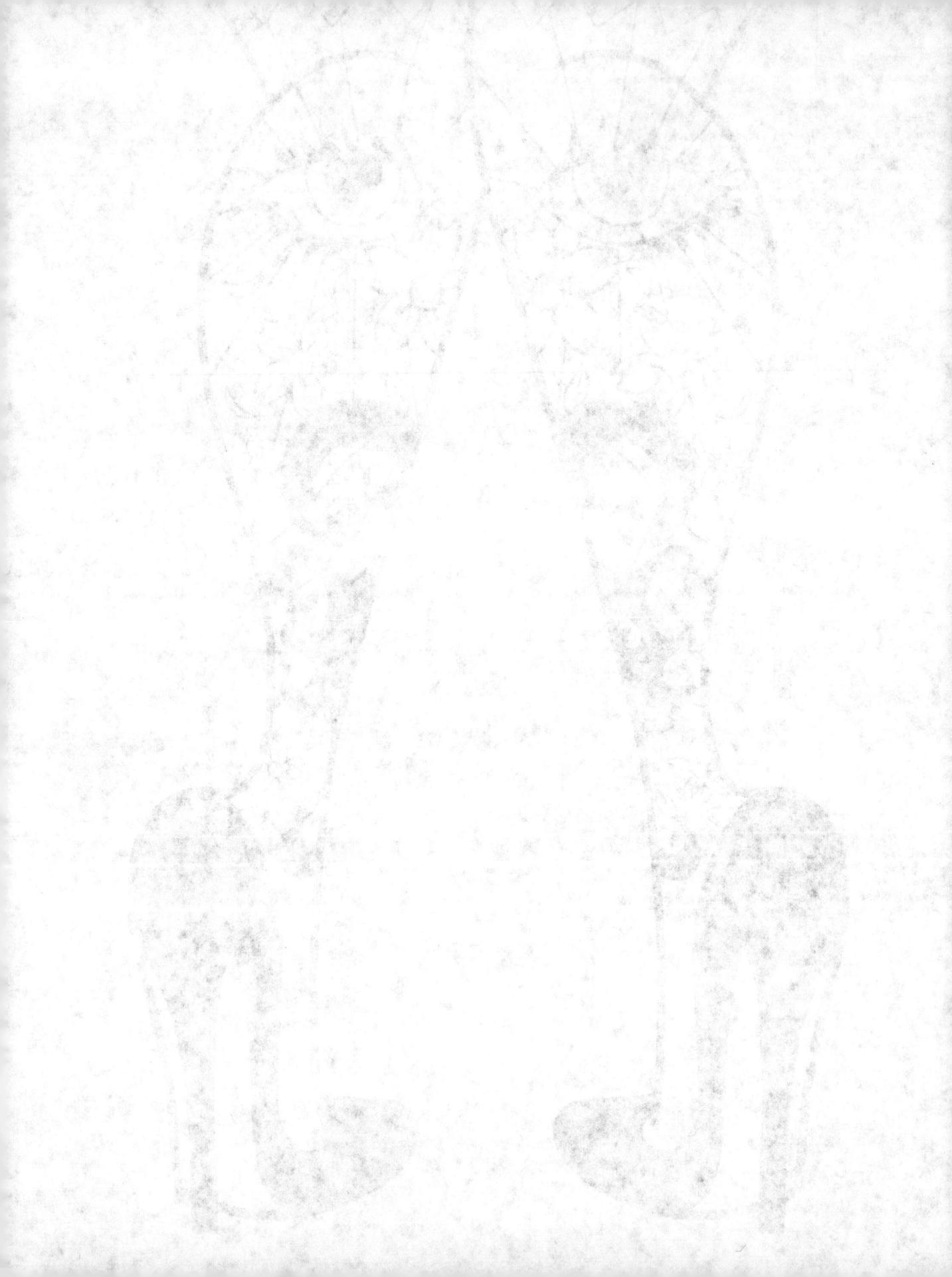

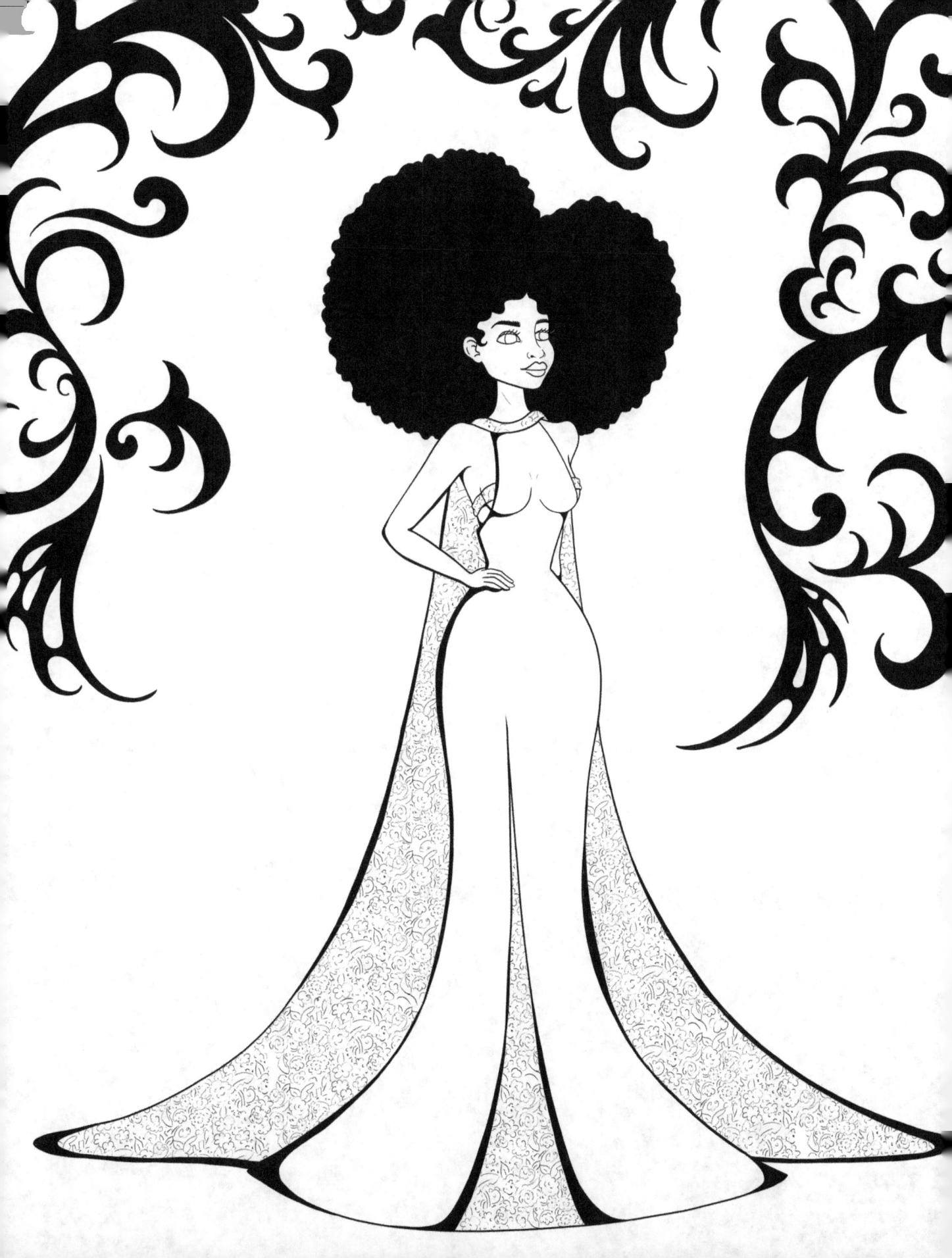

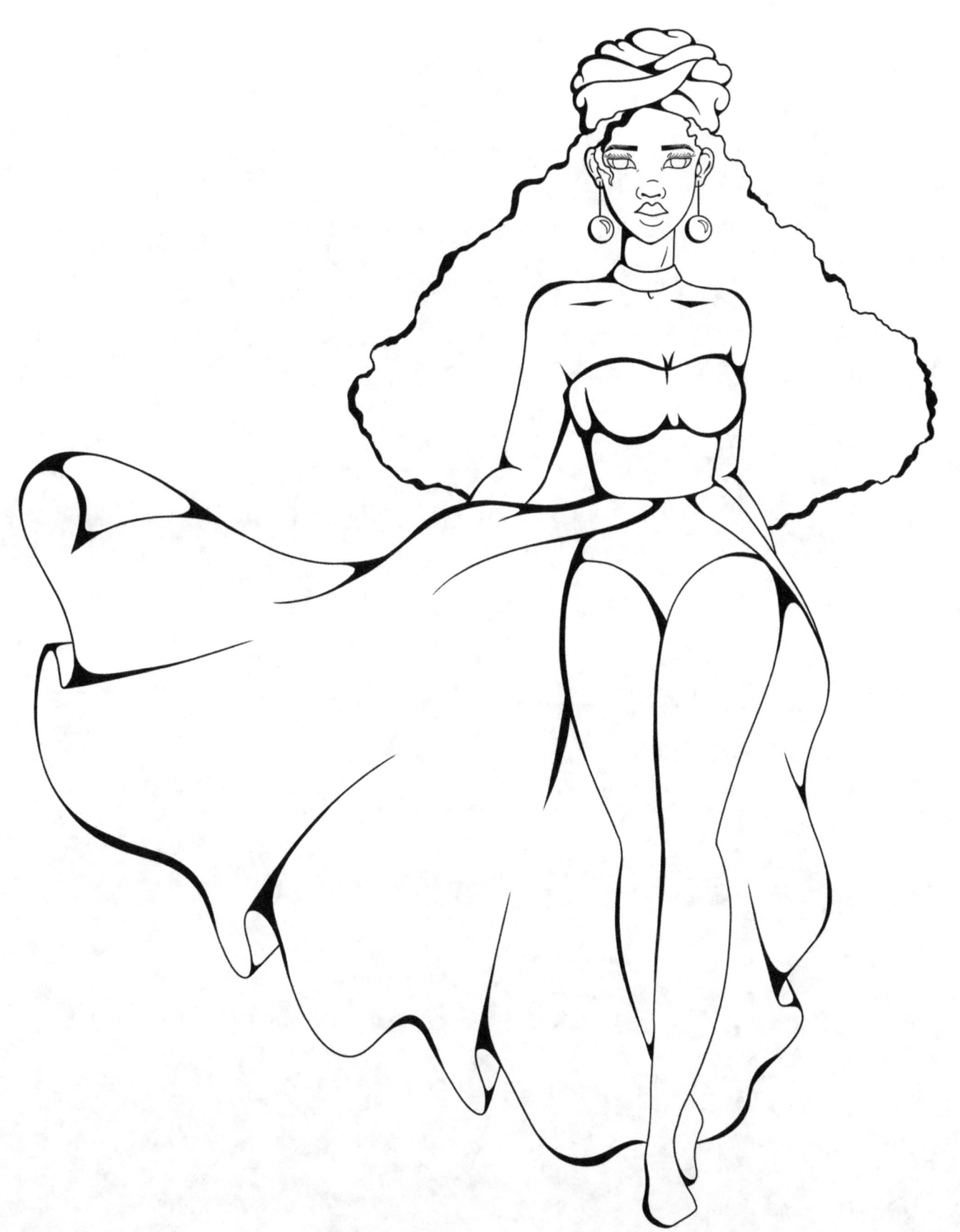

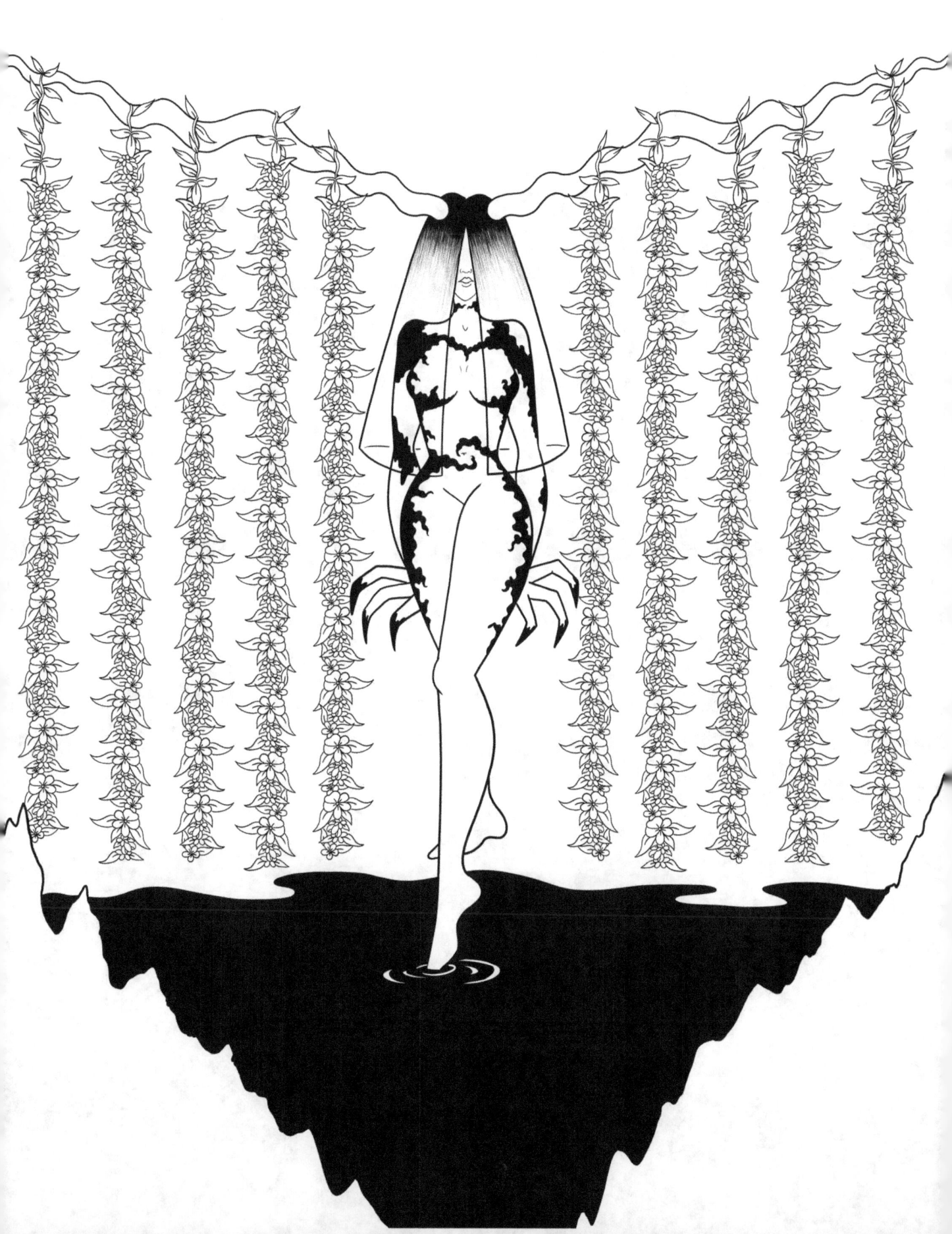

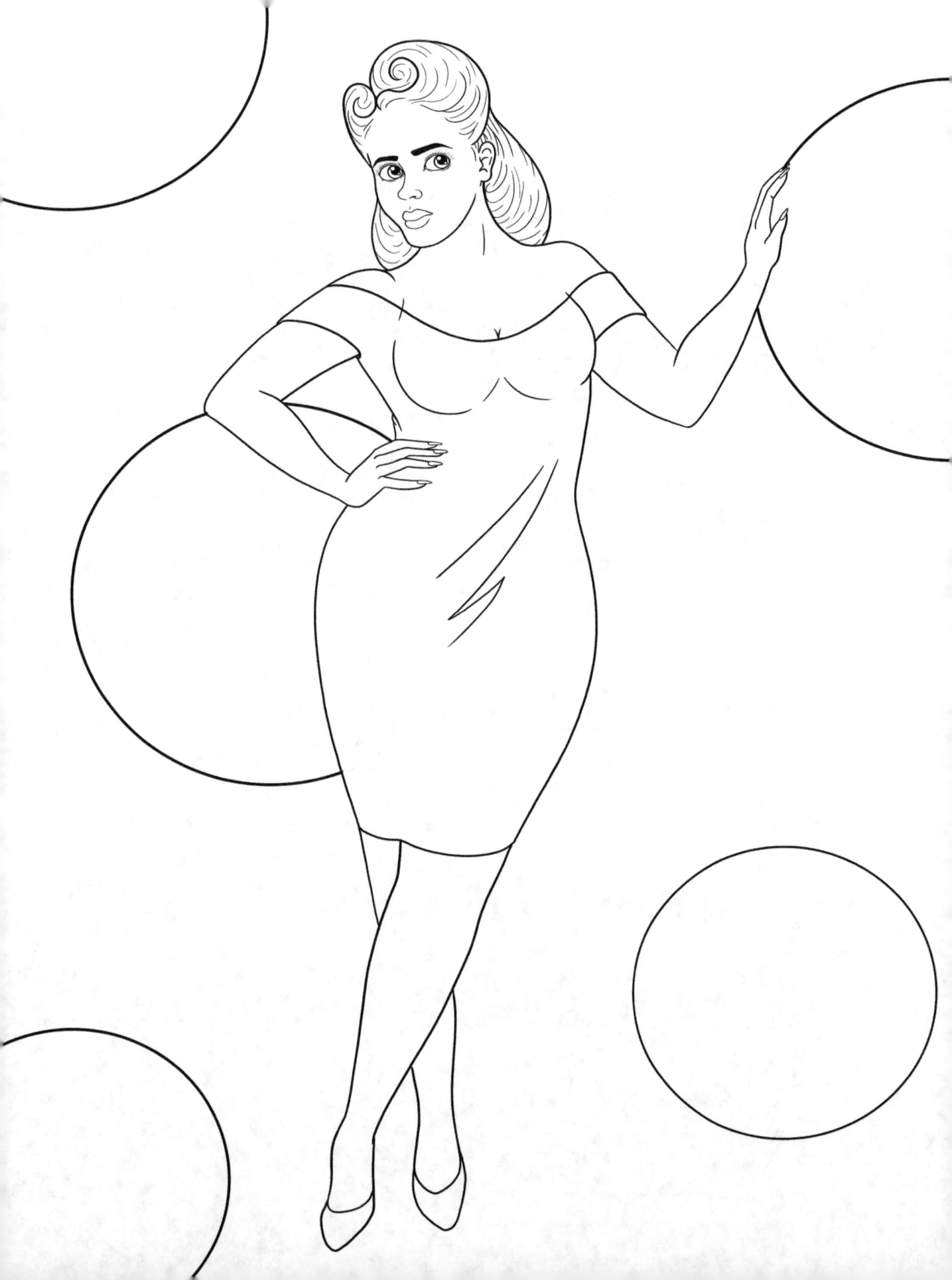

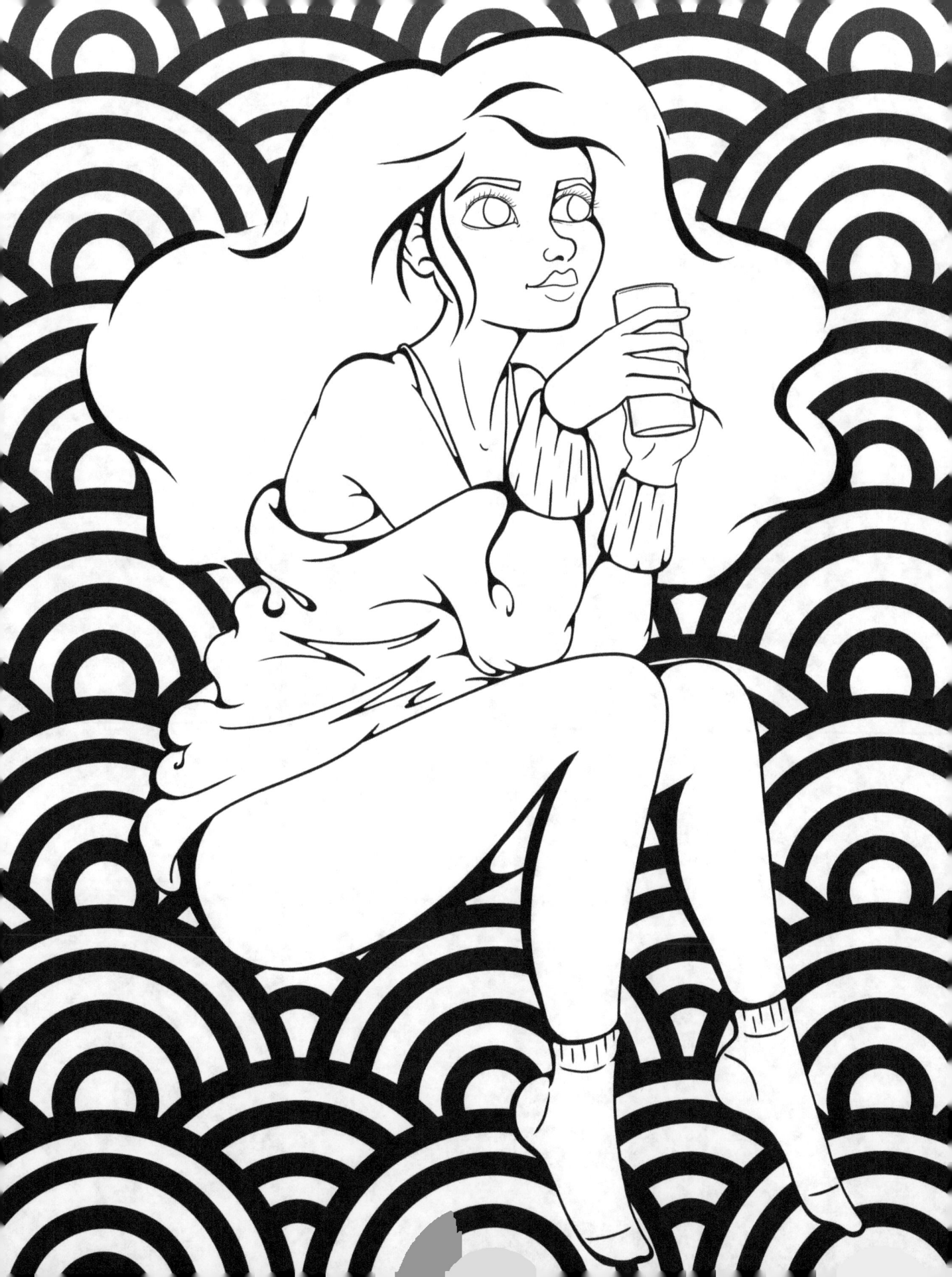

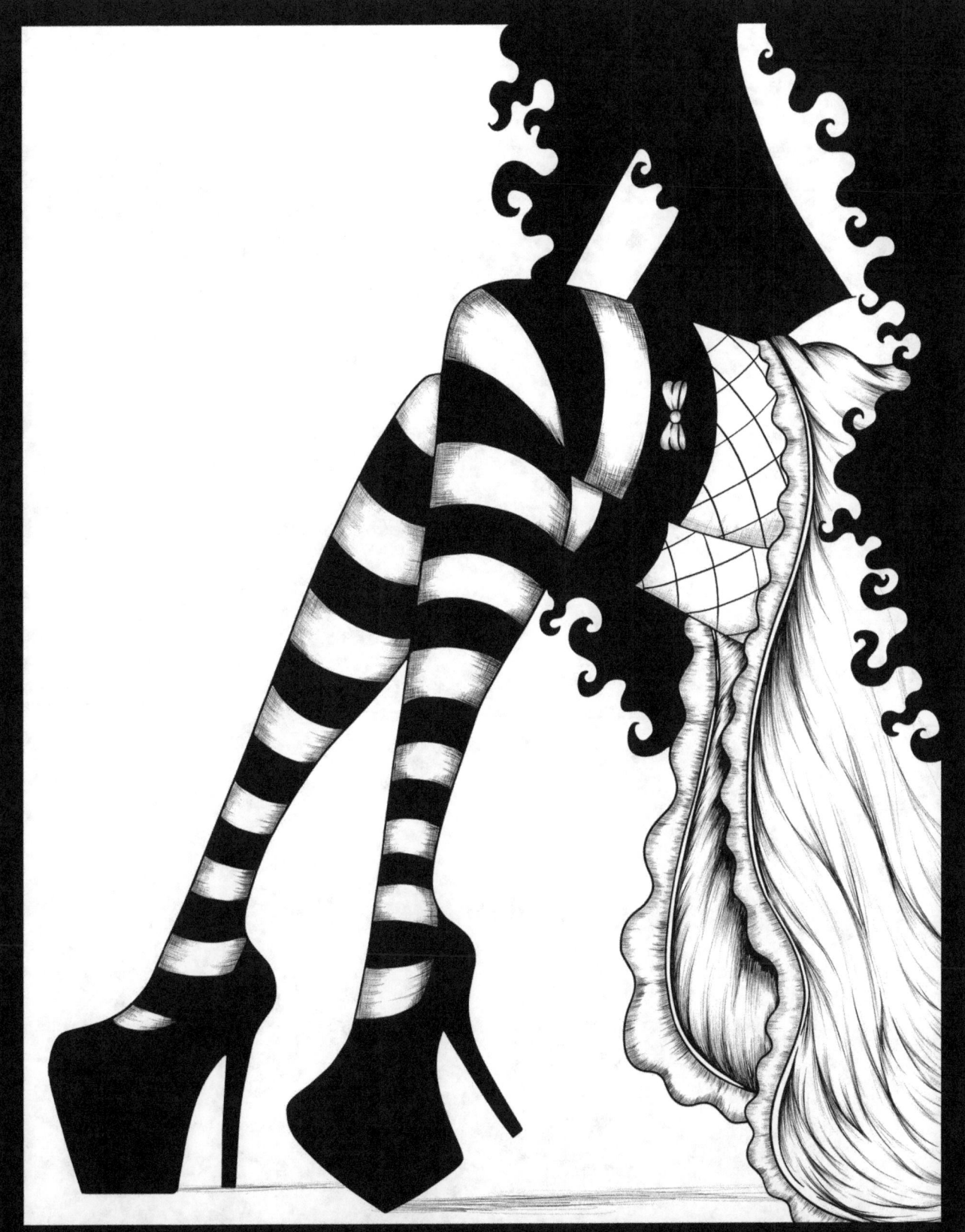

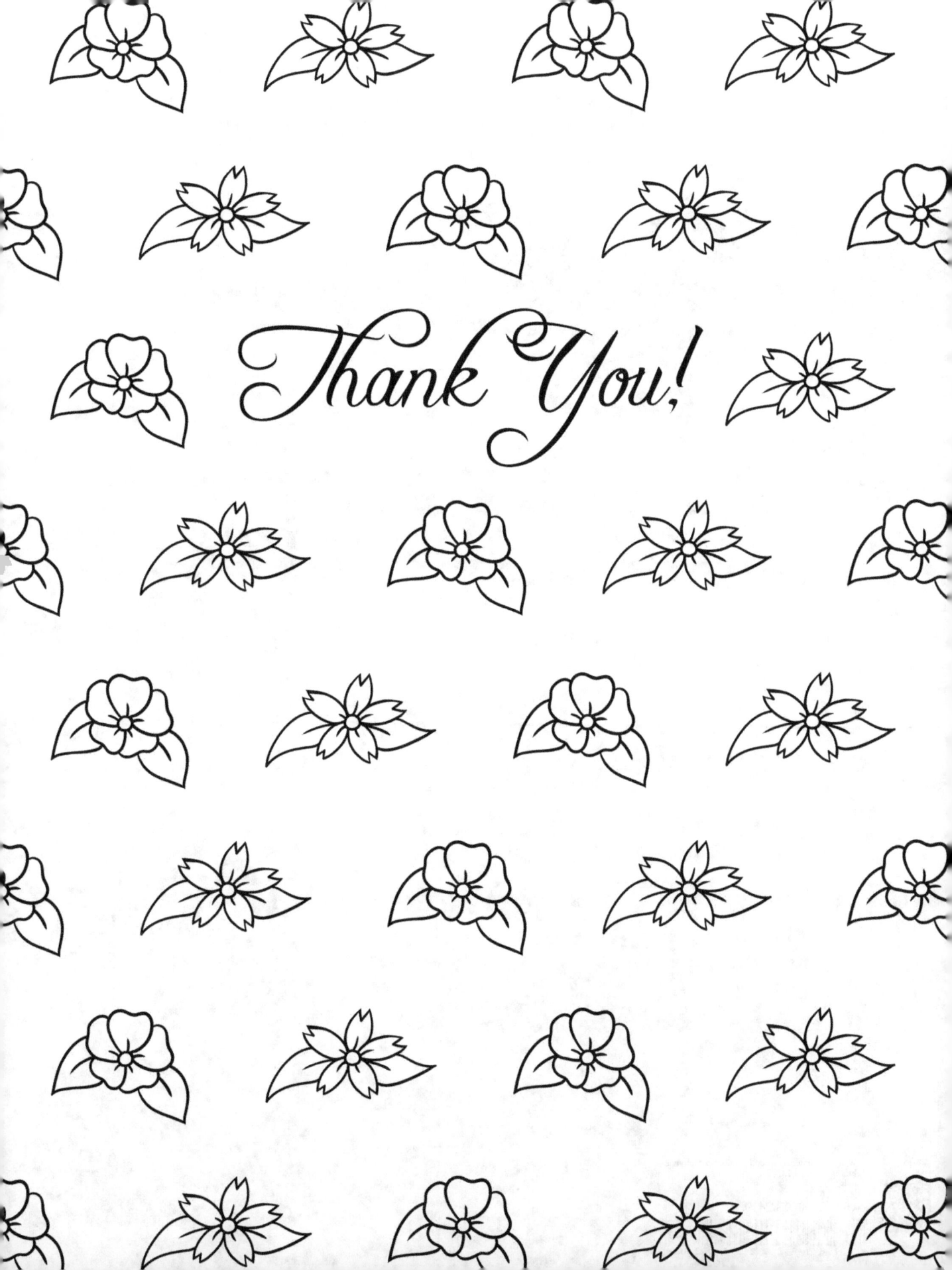

www.ingramcontent.com/pod-product-compliance
Lightning Source LLC
Chambersburg PA
CBHW081635220526
45468CB00009B/2439